#70ish, #80ish, #90ish, #100ish or More
And this book is for me!

By Kevin James Joseph McNamara
(Born in 1948 and loving it.)

Table Of Contents:

Introduction:

Appendix:

Introduction:

• Hey there, lovely reader! Get ready to dive into a book that is all about you.

In the pages that follow, we will embark on a journey through life's incredible stages, from your 70s, 80s, 90s, and beyond, and the spotlight is firmly on you. This is not just another book; it is your heartfelt companion, filled with insights and encouragement to make every moment of your life truly count.

Life is an incredible adventure, and each stage brings its own unique joys and challenges. As we celebrate your journey, whether it is the 70s, a time when you are still vibrant and full of life, or the 80s, where wisdom and experience truly shine. Perhaps it is the 90s, where you are a treasure trove of stories and lessons, or maybe the 100s and beyond, because age is just a number, and you are proving that every day.

Confidence is a superpower, and you, dear reader, possess it in abundance. We will delve into how you can embrace your age with unwavering confidence. You have earned every line on your face, and each wrinkle tells a story. It is time to wear them with pride, for they are the badges of a life well-lived.

Life is a tapestry of moments, and it is in the little things that happiness resides. We will discover together how to find joy in the everyday, whether it is savoring a warm cup of tea on a rainy morning, sharing laughter with friends, or witnessing a breathtaking sunset. Your journey is peppered with these moments; let us cherish them.

Challenges are a part of life, but so is your resilience. We will explore how to conquer life's obstacles, no matter how daunting they may seem. Your life's journey has equipped you with the tools to overcome adversity, and we will uncover the strength within you to face any challenge head-on.

This book is not just about reflection; it is about growth. We will equip you with practical tools to continue evolving, learning, and thriving. From nurturing your physical and mental well-being to embracing new skills and passions, your journey is a constant opportunity for personal growth.

Life becomes richer when shared with others. We will discuss how unity and inclusivity can bring a sense of community into your life. You are a vital part of a diverse world, and your experiences and stories have the power to connect and inspire others.

As we journey together through these pages, we will reach a moment of reflection. You will have the opportunity to pause and ponder your incredible journey. Your life is a tapestry woven with experiences, and it is worth taking a moment to appreciate the beauty of it all.

Your story is unique and valuable. We will explore ways to share your experiences, not just within the pages of this book but with friends and loved ones. Your words have the potential to inspire positive change in the lives of others.

The final chapter of our journey will invite you to take action. Your wisdom and experiences are a source of inspiration, and we will discuss how you can use them to make a difference in the lives of those around you. Your journey is not just about personal growth; it is about the positive ripple effect you can create.

In this book, every word, every thought, and every page is dedicated to you, dear reader. Your life is a masterpiece in progress, and together, we will celebrate, learn, and grow. So, let us turn the page and begin this extraordinary journey, one filled with love, wisdom, and the boundless potential of age.

- **This book is not just a passive read; it is your companion on your unique journey.**

As you turn its pages, you will discover that it is not a one-way conversation but a dialogue, a partnership between you and the wisdom it contains.

Your Journey, Your Spotlight

Within these pages, the spotlight shines brightly on you, the reader. It is a celebration of your life, regardless of your age. Whether you find yourself in your 70s, 80s, 90s, or beyond, this book recognizes the significance of every moment and experience.

Embrace Confidence at Every Age

Confidence is not reserved for the young; it is a superpower that you possess abundantly. We will explore how to embrace your age with unwavering confidence. Those lines on your face? They are earned badges of a life rich with stories and wisdom. It is time to wear them with pride.

Discovering Joy in Everyday Moments

Happiness resides in the simplicity of everyday moments, whether it is the aroma of morning coffee, the laughter of loved ones, or the beauty of a sunset. Your journey is brimming with these treasures, and this book serves as your guide to finding joy in them.

Conquering Life's Challenges

Life's challenges are woven into its tapestry, but so is your resilience. We will dive into strategies for conquering life's obstacles, regardless of their daunting nature. Your life journey has equipped you with the tools to triumph over adversity, and we are here to help you unearth the strength within you.

Equipped for Tangible Growth

This book is not solely about reflection; it is a practical guide for tangible growth. We will unveil practical tools to aid your continuous evolution, learning, and flourishing. From nurturing your physical and mental well-being to embracing new skills and passions, your journey remains an ongoing opportunity for personal growth.

Fostering Unity and Inclusivity

Life gains depth when shared with others. We will explore how unity and inclusivity can infuse a sense of community into your life. You are an essential part of a diverse world, and your experiences and stories hold the power to connect and inspire others.

Moments of Reflection

As we navigate this journey together, you will encounter moments of reflection. Take a pause and contemplate your remarkable journey. Your life forms a tapestry woven with experiences, and it is worth taking a moment to appreciate its beauty.

Sharing Your Unique Story

Your story is a precious and distinct one. We will suggest various ways to share your experiences, not only within the confines of this book but also with friends and loved ones. Your words possess the potential to ignite positive change in the lives of others.

Inspiring Positive Change

Our final chapter will extend an invitation to take action. Your wisdom and experiences serve as a source of inspiration, and we will explore how you can employ them to make a meaningful difference in the lives of those around you. Your journey is not solely about personal growth; it is about creating a ripple effect of positivity.

In this book, every word, every thought, and every page is dedicated to you, dear reader. Your life is a masterpiece in progress, and together, we will celebrate, learn, and grow. So, let us embark on this extraordinary journey, one filled with love, wisdom, and the boundless potential of age.

• Don't forget your favorite pen and a pad of paper; you will want to jot down your thoughts.

In the hustle and bustle of our fast-paced lives, we often find ourselves inundated with information, racing against time, and caught up in the digital whirlwind that surrounds us. It is easy to overlook the simple yet profound act of putting pen to paper. But amidst the digital age, where screens and keyboards dominate our daily interactions, the humble pen and paper remain steadfast companions, ready to offer us a myriad of benefits that are worth celebrating and rediscovering.

The invitation to remember your favorite pen and a pad of paper is an invitation to reconnect with a timeless practice that transcends generations. It is a gentle nudge to slow down, to pause and reflect, and to embrace the therapeutic art of writing. In a world where efficiency often takes precedence, taking a moment to write by hand may seem like a quaint choice, but it is a choice that can enrich our lives in numerous ways.

First and foremost, writing with a pen on paper fosters a sense of mindfulness. As you sit down with your chosen tools, you enter a state of presence. The act of forming each letter and word requires your full attention. The deliberate strokes of the pen across the page ground you in the moment, allowing you to escape the distractions and noise of the digital realm. It is a meditative practice that encourages you to be fully engaged with your thoughts, feelings, and ideas.

Moreover, writing by hand has a unique tactile quality that engages your senses. The feel of the pen in your hand, the texture of the paper beneath your fingertips, and the gentle sound of the nib gliding across the page create a sensory experience that is both comforting and intimate. It is a tangible connection to your thoughts and emotions, one that digital devices often lack.

Your favorite pen, chosen for its weight, ink flow, or sentimental value, becomes an extension of yourself. It becomes a trusted companion on your journey of self-expression. Each stroke of the pen is a reflection of your individuality, and the ink on the page carries the essence of your unique voice.

In the act of writing, you have the freedom to explore your innermost thoughts and emotions without the constraints of character limits or the distractions of notifications. Your pad of paper becomes a safe space where you can pour out your heart, jot down your dreams, or simply record the events of your day. It is a canvas for creativity, a repository for memories, and a tool for problem-solving.

Additionally, the act of writing by hand has cognitive benefits that extend beyond the act itself. Studies have shown that it can enhance learning and retention. When you take notes by hand, you are more likely to synthesize and internalize information, leading to a deeper understanding of the subject matter. It is a powerful tool for students and lifelong learners alike.

Furthermore, writing with a pen and paper can be a source of solace and catharsis. Whether you are journaling your thoughts, expressing gratitude, or working through challenging emotions, the physical act of writing can be therapeutic. It allows you to release pent-up feelings, gain clarity, and find closure.

Your favorite pen and pad of paper are also versatile companions. They are always at your disposal, ready to capture your ideas whenever inspiration strikes. Whether you are sketching a spontaneous drawing, jotting down a brilliant idea, or composing a heartfelt letter, they are the tools of spontaneity and creativity.

In a world where digital communication often lacks the personal touch of handwritten messages, receiving a heartfelt note written in ink can be a profound and cherished experience for both the sender and the recipient. Your handwritten words carry a warmth and authenticity that digital messages cannot replicate. They become keepsakes, treasured reminders of your thoughtfulness and care.

In essence, the simple act of remembering your favorite pen and a pad of paper is an invitation to slow down, to reconnect with yourself, and to savor the beauty of the analog world in an increasingly digital age. It is an acknowledgment of the enduring power of the written word, a timeless practice that continues to enrich our lives in countless ways.

So, as you embark on your daily adventures, whether it is a meeting, a journey, or a moment of reflection, do not forget to tuck your favorite pen and a pad of paper into your bag or pocket. They are your allies in the quest for mindfulness, creativity, self-expression, and connection. They are the keys to unlocking the transformative magic of putting pen to paper, one stroke at a time.

- **And when you discover gems, make sure to share them with your friends – they will appreciate it!**

In the vast landscape of our lives, we often come across moments, experiences, and insights that shimmer like precious gems. These are the moments when we stumble upon something extraordinary, whether it is a profound thought, a hidden talent, a beautiful place, a heartwarming story, or a piece of wisdom that resonates with our souls. These gems have the power to enrich our lives, inspire us, and create connections with others.

The invitation to share these gems with your friends is a reminder of the joy that comes from spreading positivity and the profound impact that sharing can have on our relationships. It is an acknowledgment of the value of these shared treasures and the bonds they can create among friends.

Imagine, for a moment, that you have uncovered a beautiful gem during your life's journey. It could be a breathtaking sunrise you witnessed during a morning walk, a powerful quote that deeply resonated with you, a new skill or hobby you have developed, or a heartwarming act of kindness you witnessed. These gems are not meant to be hoarded; they are meant to be shared and celebrated.

Sharing these moments of wonder and insight with your friends is an act of generosity and connection. It is a way of extending an open hand and saying, "I've found something special, and I want you to experience it too." It is a gesture of love, friendship, and camaraderie.

When you share a gem with your friends, you are not just relaying information; you are offering a piece of yourself. You are sharing a part of your heart and soul, something that has touched you on a deep level. In doing so, you create a bridge of understanding and empathy between yourself and your friends. You invite them to see the world through your eyes, to feel what you felt, and to be a part of your inner world.

Sharing gems also fosters a sense of gratitude and appreciation. When you take the time to share something beautiful or meaningful with your friends, you are expressing your gratitude for having them in your life. You are saying, "I value our friendship, and I want to share moments of joy and inspiration with you." This act of appreciation strengthens the bonds of friendship and deepens the sense of connection.

Moreover, sharing gems can be a source of inspiration for your friends. It has the power to spark their curiosity, ignite their passions, or uplift their spirits. Your act of sharing can lead to a chain reaction of positive experiences and personal growth. It is a way of paying forward to the beauty and wisdom you have encountered in your own life.

Consider the ripple effect of sharing. When you share a gem with your friends, they, in turn, may be inspired to share their own discoveries with you and others. This exchange of treasures creates a rich tapestry of shared experiences and insights, enriching the lives of all involved. It is a beautiful cycle of giving and receiving that enhances the quality of our friendships and the depth of our connections.

Sharing gems also contributes to the collective well-being of your social circle. It fosters a culture of positivity, appreciation, and mutual support. It reminds everyone that life is filled with moments of beauty and wonder, even amidst the challenges. By sharing these gems, you contribute to creating a more uplifting and optimistic environment for yourself and your friends.

Furthermore, sharing gems with your friends strengthens your role as a source of inspiration and positivity in their lives. It positions you as someone who values and celebrates the beauty and wisdom that can be found in everyday life. Your friends are likely to appreciate your thoughtfulness and may turn to you for inspiration and encouragement in the future.

In essence, sharing gems with your friends is a gesture of love, a celebration of the beauty and wisdom that life has to offer, and an affirmation of the bonds of friendship. It is an act that brings joy, inspiration, and connection to both the giver and the receiver. So, the next time you discover a gem in your life's journey, whether it is a profound insight or a simple moment of joy, do not hesitate to share it with your friends. They will not only appreciate it but also treasure the beautiful connection it creates among kindred spirits.

Chapter 1: Embrace Your Age with Confidence

• Feel free to embrace this chapter with the confidence that it is here to boost your spirits.

Age, they say, is just a number, and indeed it is. Yet, in a world that often glorifies youth and associates it with beauty and vitality, embracing your age with confidence can sometimes be a challenge. But, dear reader, you possess a superpower that transcends the boundaries of time – the power of confidence. In this book, we embark on a journey to explore how you can embrace your age with unwavering confidence, recognizing that every line on your face is a badge of a life well-lived.

Embracing your age is not about denying the passage of time or attempting to turn back the clock. It is about celebrating the unique journey that has brought you to this moment. It is about acknowledging the wisdom, experiences, and stories that are etched into your being. It is about understanding that with age comes a reservoir of knowledge and a perspective that only time can bestow.

Confidence is not reserved for the young; it is a quality that transcends age. In fact, it is a superpower that often grows stronger with each passing year. With age comes a deeper understanding of oneself, a greater acceptance of imperfections, and a heightened sense of self-assuredness. It is as if life has been your tutor, and the lessons it has imparted have enriched your confidence.

Think about it – you have navigated through various stages of life, overcoming challenges, experiencing joys, and accumulating a treasure trove of memories. Each of these experiences has contributed to the tapestry of your life and has shaped you into the unique individual you are today. Your age is not something to hide or be ashamed of; it is something to embrace proudly.

As you look in the mirror and see the lines and wrinkles that time has etched upon your face, remember that these are not signs of weakness or decay; they are symbols of strength, resilience, and character. Each line tells a story – a story of laughter, of tears, of triumphs, and of lessons learned. These lines are your medals of honor, earned through the journey of life.

Embracing your age with confidence also means recognizing the beauty that comes with maturity. There is a grace and elegance that accompanies the passage of time. It is the radiance of a soul that has weathered storms and emerged stronger. It is the allure of wisdom and depth that can only come from a life well-lived.

Moreover, confidence in your age empowers you to set an example for others. It sends a powerful message to those around you that age is not a limitation but an asset. It encourages younger generations to embrace their own journeys and value the wisdom that comes with the passing of time. Your confidence becomes an inspiration, a beacon of hope for those who may fear growing older.

In this book, we will explore practical steps to boost your confidence and embrace your age with open arms. We will delve into self-care practices that nourish both your body and soul, enhancing your overall well-being. We will chat about the importance of self-acceptance and self-love, as these are the foundations of true confidence.

We will also touch upon the significance of setting goals and pursuing passions at any age. Age should never be a barrier to dreaming big or embarking on new adventures. Your journey is a continuous opportunity for personal growth and fulfillment.

Additionally, we will address the role of perspective and mindset in bolstering your confidence. How you perceive your age and the beliefs you hold about it can significantly impact your self-esteem. By adopting a positive and empowering perspective, you can increase your confidence.

Throughout this book, we will draw upon real-life stories and insights from individuals who have embraced their age with confidence and found fulfillment in doing so. Their experiences serve as powerful examples of the transformative power of confidence and self-acceptance.

So, dear reader, as we journey through this book, remember that embracing your age with confidence is not a mere aspiration – it is a celebration of who you are and all that you have become. It is a declaration that you are proud of the life you have lived, and you are excited about the chapters yet to unfold. It is a testament to the fact that you are a masterpiece in progress, and age is but one brushstroke in the portrait of your extraordinary life.

• As you read, pause for a moment, and think about how embracing your unique stage of life is so meaningful for you and can actually change you in better ways.

Life is an intricate tapestry woven from the threads of time and experience. Each of us, as we journey through life, adds our own unique color, texture, and pattern to this grand tapestry. It is a masterpiece in progress, constantly evolving and reflecting the chapters of our existence.

In this book, we invite you to delve into the profound significance of embracing your unique stage of life, whether you find yourself in your 70s, 80s, 90s, or even beyond. It is a celebration of the remarkable journey you have undertaken and a testament to the wisdom and insights that come with the passage of time.

Embracing your age and your specific stage of life is not merely a passive acknowledgment of the years that have gone by. It is an active and transformative process that can enrich your life in ways you may not have imagined. It is about recognizing that each stage of life carries its own unique beauty, meaning, and purpose.

In a world that often emphasizes youth and measures success by arbitrary standards, it is easy to overlook the profound value of aging gracefully and embracing the gifts that come with it. But, dear reader, within your unique stage of life lies the potential for profound personal growth, self-discovery, and the opportunity to make a lasting impact on the world around you.

Think about it – you have accumulated a wealth of experiences, insights, and lessons over the years. Your journey-five journey has been a repository of stories, both joyful and challenging, that have shaped you into the extraordinary individual you are today. Each moment, each triumph, and each setback has contributed to the masterpiece that is your life.

Embracing your unique stage of life means recognizing that age is not a limitation but a wellspring of wisdom. It is a time to draw from the deep well of your experiences and share the valuable lessons you have learned with others. Your unique perspective on life, forged through decades of living, has the power to inspire, guide, and uplift those who cross your path.

Moreover, embracing your age is an act of self-empowerment. It is about understanding that your worth and value are not determined by the number of years you have lived but by the depth of your character, the richness of your experiences, and the impact you can have on the world. It is a declaration that you are not defined by society's arbitrary standards of youth but by your own authenticity and the beauty of your journey.

As you embrace your unique stage of life, consider how it can change you in profoundly positive ways. It offers you the opportunity to shed societal expectations and embrace your true self. It encourages self-reflection, self-acceptance, and self-love – essential ingredients for a fulfilling and meaningful life.

Throughout this book, we will explore the transformative power of embracing your unique stage of life. We will delve into practical strategies for self-discovery, personal growth, and finding purpose in every moment. We will celebrate the beauty of aging and the incredible potential it holds.

We will also share stories of individuals who have embraced their unique stages of life and discovered newfound vitality, purpose, and joy. Their experiences serve as a testament to the profound impact that embracing your age can have on your overall well-being and happiness.

So, as you read these pages, allow yourself to immerse yourself in the idea that embracing your unique stage of life is not just a passive acknowledgment but an active choice that can change you in better ways. It is a celebration of your individuality, a recognition of your worth, and an invitation to live life to its fullest, no matter how many candles adorn your birthday cake.

Your unique stage of life is a precious gift, and within it lies the potential for transformation, growth, and fulfillment. As you embark on this journey of self-discovery and embrace the beauty of aging, remember that you are the author of your own narrative, and every chapter is an opportunity to shine brightly and leave an indelible mark on the world.

So, dear reader, let these words resonate within you as you turn the pages of this book. **"Embrace your unique stage of life with an open heart and a curious mind, for it has the power to change you in ways that are both meaningful and profound."**

• Share your newfound confidence with family and friends who might benefit from a little boost; then write down how you might have helped them.

Confidence, that intangible quality that radiates from within, has the power to transform not only our own lives but also the lives of those around us. As we journey through the pages of this book, you will discover how embracing your unique stage of life and nurturing your confidence can be a beacon of light for your family and friends. It is not just about personal growth; it is about the ripple effect of positivity and inspiration that you can create.

Confidence is like a torch that illuminates the path for others. When you exude self-assuredness, it has a way of inspiring those in your circle, showing them that self-belief and self-love are attainable at any age. Your confidence becomes a source of hope, a reminder that it is never too late to embark on a journey of self-discovery and empowerment.

Think about the people in your life – your family, your friends, your loved ones. Have you ever noticed how your own confidence can influence their outlook? When you carry yourself with assurance, it can boost their spirits, elevate their self-esteem, and encourage them to embrace their own unique journeys. Your confidence becomes a gift you share with those you care about.

In this chapter, we will explore the profound impact you can have on the lives of your family and friends through the gift of confidence. We will delve into practical strategies for nurturing their self-belief and helping them recognize their own worth. We will discuss the power of positive influence and how your journey of self-confidence can serve as an inspiration to others.

As you share your newfound confidence with your family and friends, consider the ways in which you can help them along their own paths of self-discovery and empowerment. Write down your thoughts and reflections on the positive changes you may have facilitated in their lives. Your actions and words have the potential to be a guiding light, and by documenting your experiences, you can gain deeper insight into the impact you have had.

Confidence is contagious, and your own journey toward embracing your unique stage of life can be a catalyst for transformation within your social circles. It is about more than just personal growth; it is about the meaningful connections you foster and the positive change you inspire.

Throughout this chapter, we will explore the following key areas:

1. **The Ripple Effect of Confidence:** Understanding how your confidence can influence those around you and create a positive ripple effect in your social circles.

2. **Practical Strategies for Empowerment:** Exploring actionable steps to nurture the confidence of your family and friends, helping them recognize their unique worth and potential.

3. **The Power of Positive Influence:** Examining how your own journey of self-confidence can serve as a powerful source of inspiration to those you care about.

4. **Documenting Impact:** Reflecting on the ways in which you have helped your loved ones boost their confidence and achieve personal growth.

5. **Celebrating Shared Journeys:** Recognizing the beauty of supporting one another in the pursuit of self-discovery and empowerment.

As you read these pages, allow yourself to envision the positive changes you can bring into the lives of your family and friends by sharing your newfound confidence. Consider how your journey has the power to uplift and inspire those you hold dear and embrace the role you can play in helping them embark on their own paths of self-belief and self-discovery.

Your confidence is a beacon of hope, a guiding light, and a source of inspiration. **"It's time to share this invaluable gift with those who matter most to you, leaving a lasting legacy of empowerment and positivity."**

UNLOCKING
"THE GOOD"

Chapter 2: Unlocking 'The Good'

• This chapter is all about finding and savoring life's positives. Feel free to smile or laugh while you read. Write down more of the highlights of your life at this point.

Life is a tapestry woven with threads of both joy and sorrow, and within its intricate design, there are moments that shine like bright stars in the night sky. In this chapter, we invite you to embark on a journey of discovery, a journey that celebrates the simple yet profound joys that adorn the canvas of your life.

As you read these pages, allow yourself to smile, to laugh, and to relish the beauty of life's positives. It is a celebration of the small victories, the heartwarming moments, and the everyday blessings that make life truly special.

In a world that often emphasizes the pursuit of grand achievements and monumental milestones, it is easy to overlook the significance of finding and savoring life's positives in the ordinary moments. But, dear reader, within the fabric of your daily existence lies a treasure trove of happiness waiting to be unearthed.

Think about it – the aroma of your morning coffee, the gentle warmth of the sun on your skin, the laughter of loved ones, the soothing sound of rain on your windowpane – these are the simple pleasures that color your life. They are the highlights of your everyday existence, the moments that bring a smile to your face and fill your heart with contentment.

In this chapter, we will explore the art of finding and savoring life's positives with mindfulness and intention. We will delve into practical strategies for cultivating gratitude, embracing 'the present moment', and nurturing a positive outlook on life. We will discuss the transformative power of optimism and how it can enhance your overall well-being.

As you read, take a moment to reflect on the highlights of your life at this point. Write them down, cherish them, and allow them to serve as reminders of the beauty that surrounds you. Your life is a rich tapestry of experiences, and within its threads are the gems of happiness that deserve to be treasured.

Throughout this chapter, we will explore the following key areas:

1. **The Art of Gratitude:** Discovering the profound impact of gratitude on your overall happiness and well-being.

2. **Embracing the Present Moment:** Learning to be fully present and mindful, allowing you to savor life's positives as they unfold.

3. **The Power of Optimism:** Exploring how a positive outlook on life can enhance your resilience and overall quality of life.

4. **Cultivating Joy:** Uncovering practical strategies for finding and savoring the simple pleasures that bring happiness to your daily life.

5. **Reflecting on Highlights:** Taking time to write down and reflect on the highlights of your life at this point, celebrating the moments that have brought you joy.

As you journey through these pages, immerse yourself in the delightful task of finding and savoring life's positives. Let this chapter be a source of inspiration, reminding you that happiness is not solely found in grand achievements but also in the everyday moments that fill your heart with warmth and laughter.

Your life is a collection of beautiful moments waiting to be acknowledged and celebrated. So, dear reader, read with a smile on your face, for this chapter is a celebration of the joy that resides within you and the boundless beauty of life's simple pleasures.

• Discover joy, fulfillment, and meaning, and jot down the moments that make your hear

Life is a grand tapestry, and within its intricate design, there are threads of joy, fulfillment, and meaning waiting to be discovered. In this chapter, we have embarked on a journey to explore the profound significance of uncovering the moments that make your heart sing.

As you read these pages, allow yourself to immerse yourself in the beauty of life's joyful moments. It is a celebration of the experiences that fill your heart with happiness, the moments that bring a sense of fulfillment, and the deep, meaningful connections that give life its purpose.

In a world that often rushes by, it is easy to overlook the simple yet profound moments that infuse your life with joy and meaning. But, dear reader, within the fabric of your existence are treasures waiting to be unearthed – moments that have the power to transform your perspective and enrich your journey.

Think about it – the laughter of loved ones, the feeling of accomplishment after a challenging task, the beauty of a vibrant sunset, the warmth of a hug from a friend – these are the moments that elevate your spirit and remind you of the beauty of being alive.

In this chapter, we will explore the art of discovering joy, fulfillment, and meaning with mindfulness and intention. We will delve into practical strategies for cultivating a sense of purpose, fostering deep connections with others, and finding fulfillment in both small and significant moments.

As you read, take a moment to jot down the moments that make your heart sing, the experiences that resonate with your soul, and the connections that bring meaning to your life. Your journey is a collection of these moments, and they deserve to be acknowledged and cherished.

Throughout this chapter, we will explore the following key areas:

1. **The Pursuit of Purpose:** Discovering how a sense of purpose can infuse your life with meaning and fulfillment.

2. **The Beauty of Connection:** Exploring the profound significance of deep and meaningful connections with others, and how they enrich your journey.

3. **Moments of Fulfillment:** Uncovering practical strategies for finding fulfillment in both everyday experiences and significant milestones.

4. **Mindful Joy:** Embracing the practice of mindfulness to fully savor the moments that make your heart sing.

5. **Reflection and Gratitude:** Taking time to jot down and reflect on the moments that have brought you joy, fulfillment, and meaning, celebrating the beauty of your unique journey.

As you journey through these pages, immerse yourself in the delightful task of discovering the moments that make your heart sing. Let this chapter be a source of inspiration, reminding you that joy, fulfillment, and meaning are not distant aspirations but integral parts of your everyday life.

Your life is a collection of beautiful moments waiting to be acknowledged and celebrated. So, dear reader, **read with an open heart, for this chapter is a celebration of the profound beauty that resides within you and the boundless potential for joy, fulfillment, and meaning that exists in each moment.**

• Share your happiness with friends because sharing joy is the best kind of gift.

Share your happiness with friends because sharing joy is the best kind of gift.

Happiness is a radiant emotion that has the power to brighten not only our own lives but also the lives of those around us. In this chapter, we dive into the art of sharing happiness, recognizing that by spreading joy to friends, we create a positive and uplifting ripple effect.

As you journey through the pages of this chapter, allow yourself to immerse yourself in the delightful task of sharing your happiness with friends. It is a celebration of the connections you hold dear, the moments of laughter and companionship, and the simple yet profound act of bringing joy into each other's lives.

Friendship is a treasured bond that enriches our existence. It is a source of support, laughter, and shared experiences. Your friends are the individuals who stand by your side through life's ups and downs, and they are the ones who bring warmth and companionship to your journey.

Think about it – the moments of shared laughter, the heartfelt conversations, the celebrations of achievements, and the comfort during challenging times – these are the threads that weave the tapestry of friendship. They are the moments of connection and joy that create lasting memories.

In this chapter, we will explore the art of sharing happiness with friends with intention and mindfulness. We will delve into practical strategies for nurturing your friendships, fostering a sense of camaraderie, and spreading joy in ways both big and small.

As you read, reflect on the special moments you have shared with your friends and the happiness you have experienced together. Consider how you can continue to cultivate and strengthen these connections, making them even more vibrant and meaningful.

Throughout this chapter, we will explore the following key areas:

1. **The Beauty of Friendship:** Celebrating the profound significance of friendship in our lives and recognizing the value of shared moments.

2. **Nurturing Connections:** Exploring practical strategies for nurturing and deepening your friendships, ensuring they remain a source of joy and support.

3. **The Joy of Shared Experiences:** Reflecting on the moments of happiness you have shared with friends and the positive impact they have had on your well-being.

4. **The Art of Giving:** Discovering how acts of kindness and generosity can spread happiness and strengthen your friendships.

5. **Creating Lasting Memories:** Embracing the practice of creating meaningful and lasting memories with friends, celebrating the beauty of shared experiences.

As you journey through these pages, immerse yourself in the heartwarming task of sharing your happiness with friends. Let this chapter be a reminder that the bonds of friendship are enriched through the exchange of joy and support.

Your friends are your cherished companions on life's journey, and by sharing happiness with them, you not only enhance your own well-being but also contribute to the happiness and fulfillment of those you hold dear. So, dear reader, read with a heart full of gratitude for the friendships that light up your life, and let the pages of this chapter inspire you to continue sharing joy with friends, for it is the best kind of gift.

Before you proceed, go back, and re-read this chapter and reflect on it. Go back a second time if you feel like it.

Then wait for an hour before reading the next chapter.

Chapter 3: Conquering 'The Bad'

• Dive into this chapter knowing it is here to help you tackle life's challenges head-on.

Life is a journey filled with both triumphs and trials, and in this chapter, we embark on a voyage to explore the art of conquering life's challenges with resilience and determination. As you read these pages, allow yourself to embrace the mindset that adversity is not a roadblock but a steppingstone to growth and strength.

Challenges are an integral part of the tapestry of life. They come in various forms, from personal obstacles to unexpected external circumstances, and they test our resilience and inner fortitude. But, dear reader, within every challenge lies the potential for growth and transformation.

Think about it – the challenges you have faced throughout your life have shaped you into the resilient and capable individual you are today. They have taught you valuable lessons, honed your problem-solving skills, and strengthened your determination. Each challenge, no matter how daunting, has equipped you with the tools to overcome adversity.

In this chapter, we will explore the art of conquering life's challenges with a mindset of resilience and empowerment. We will delve into practical strategies for facing adversity head-on, navigating through difficult times, and emerging stronger on the other side.

As you read, reflect on the challenges you have encountered in your own life and the valuable lessons they have taught. Consider how you can apply the principles of resilience and determination to tackle current or future challenges with confidence and grace.

Throughout this chapter, we will explore the following key areas:

1. **Embracing Resilience:** Discovering the power of resilience as a key asset in facing life's challenges and adversity.

2. **Navigating Difficult Times:** Exploring practical strategies for navigating through difficult situations, from personal setbacks to external crises.

3. **Overcoming Obstacles:** Reflecting on the lessons learned from overcoming challenges and the growth that can emerge from adversity.

4. **The Role of Support:** Recognizing the importance of a support system and seeking assistance when facing particularly challenging situations.

5. **Personal Growth:** Embracing the concept that challenges are opportunities for personal growth and transformation.

As you journey through these pages, immerse yourself in the empowering task of tackling life's challenges head-on. Let this chapter be a source of inspiration, reminding you that you possess the inner strength and resilience to overcome adversity and emerge stronger than before.

Your life is a testament to your ability to face challenges with courage and determination. So, dear reader, read with a sense of empowerment, for this chapter is a celebration of your capacity to conquer life's challenges and emerge as a stronger and more resilient individual.

• Think about your own setbacks and how the strategies you find here might help you overcome them. Write down your setbacks and what helped you.

Setbacks are a natural part of life's journey, and they often serve as valuable opportunities for growth and learning. In this chapter, we delve into the art of overcoming setbacks with resilience and determination. As you read these pages, consider how the strategies and insights presented here can help you navigate and conquer your own setbacks.

Setbacks come in various forms, from personal challenges and disappointments to unexpected twists and turns in our life paths. They can test our patience, resilience, and inner strength. However, it is essential to recognize that setbacks do not define us; it is how we respond to them that matters.

Think about it – throughout your life, you have likely encountered setbacks, both big and small. Each setback brought its unique set of challenges and required you to adapt, learn, and grow. These experiences have shaped you into the resilient individual you are today.

In this chapter, we will explore the art of overcoming setbacks with a mindset of resilience and determination. We will delve into practical strategies for navigating setbacks, learning from them, and emerging stronger on the other side.

As you read, take a moment to reflect on the setbacks you have faced in your own life and the lessons they have taught you. Consider how you can apply the principles of resilience and determination to overcome your setbacks and turn them into steppingstones toward your goals and aspirations.

Throughout this chapter, we will explore the following key areas:

1. **Understanding Setbacks:** Recognizing setbacks as part of life's journey and understanding their potential for growth and learning.

2. **Building Resilience:** Exploring strategies for developing resilience and inner strength to face setbacks with confidence.

3. **Navigating Setbacks:** Reflecting on practical approaches to navigate through setbacks, from identifying solutions to seeking support.

4. **Learning and Growth:** Embracing setbacks as opportunities for personal growth, learning, and self-improvement.

5. **Turning Setbacks into Success:** Discovering how setbacks can be transformed into steppingstones toward achieving your goals and aspirations.

As you journey through these pages, immerse yourself in the empowering task of overcoming setbacks with resilience and determination. Let this chapter be a source of inspiration, reminding you that setbacks are not roadblocks but opportunities for growth and transformation.

Your life is a testament to your ability to overcome challenges and setbacks with courage and determination. So, dear reader, **read with a sense of empowerment, for this chapter is a celebration of your** capacity to conquer setbacks and emerge stronger and wiser on your journey.

• Share your strategies, by writing about them, with friends who might be facing tough times – you could be their guiding light.

In life, we often find ourselves navigating through challenging times, and during such moments, the support and guidance of friends can be invaluable. In this section, we explore the art of offering support to friends who may be facing tough times, and we emphasize the profound impact you can have as their guiding light.

Think about it – your friends are an essential part of your life's journey, and they have likely been there for you during your own challenging moments. They provide comfort, understanding, and a sense of companionship that can make all the difference during tough times. As you read this chapter, consider how you can be a source of support and guidance to your friends when they need it most.

Friendship is a two-way street, and being a guiding light to your friends in their times of need is not only a gesture of kindness but also an opportunity to strengthen the bonds of friendship. It is a way to reciprocate the support you have received and to create a network of mutual care and understanding.

In this chapter, we will explore the art of offering support to friends with intention and compassion. We will delve into practical strategies for being there for your friends, helping them navigate through tough times, and offering a shoulder to lean on.

As you read, reflect on the moments when your friends have been there for you during challenging times and the impact it had on your well-being. Consider how you can extend the same level of care and support to your friends when they face difficulties.

Throughout this chapter, we will explore the following key areas:

1. **The Importance of Friendship:** Recognizing the profound significance of friendship and the role it plays in supporting each other through tough times.

2. **Being an Active Listener:** Learning the art of active listening and how it can provide solace and understanding to your friends.

3. **Offering Practical Assistance:** Exploring ways to offer practical assistance to friends facing challenges, from running errands to providing emotional support.

4. **Providing Emotional Comfort:** Understanding the importance of providing emotional comfort and reassurance to friends during difficult moments.

5. **Encouraging Self-Care:** Encouraging your friends to prioritize self-care and well-being and offering guidance on self-care practices.

6. **Being Non-Judgmental:** Emphasizing the importance of creating a safe and non-judgmental space for your friends to express their feelings and concerns.

As you journey through these pages, immerse yourself in the compassionate task of being a guiding light to your friends during their tough times. Let this chapter be a reminder that your support can make a significant difference in their lives and that your friendship is a source of strength and comfort.

Your friends are a cherished part of your journey, and by offering your guidance and support, you become a beacon of light in their darkest moments. So, dear reader, **read with a heart full of compassion and empathy, for this chapter celebrates the profound impact you can have as the guiding light for your friends in need.**

~ ~ ~ ~ ~

"As we conclude Chapter 3, I encourage you to pause and reflect on everything you've written up to this point. It is in this introspective moment that you will discover the real opportunities for enhancing your life.
" ~ ~ ~ ~ ~

Chapter 4: Facing 'The Ugly'

• As you read stories of triumph, remember that life's toughest moments are often the small struggles in life and are part of the journey.

Triumphs come in various forms, and often, the most significant victories in life are the result of conquering the smaller struggles along the way. In this chapter, we explore the significance of recognizing and celebrating the smaller triumphs in life, as they are an integral part of the journey towards greater achievements and fulfillment.

Think about it – as you have journeyed through life, you have encountered countless challenges, both big and small. While major accomplishments and milestones are essential, it is the smaller triumphs that often define the path to success. These smaller victories can be daily achievements, personal growth moments, or moments of overcoming obstacles that may seem inconsequential but are essential building blocks on your journey.

In this chapter, we will delve into the art of acknowledging and celebrating the small triumphs in life. We will explore why these moments matter and how they contribute to your overall sense of well-being and success. As you read, consider how you can apply the principles discussed here to appreciate and celebrate your own small triumphs.

Throughout this chapter, we will explore the following key areas:

1. **The Power of Perspective:** Understanding how your perspective can influence your perception of small triumphs and their significance.

2. **Recognizing Daily Achievements:** Learning to recognize and celebrate daily achievements, no matter how minor they may seem.

3. **Personal Growth Moments:** Reflecting on how moments of personal growth and self-improvement are often small triumphs that pave the way for greater success.

4. **Overcoming Everyday Obstacles:** Exploring how overcoming everyday obstacles contributes to resilience and determination.

5. **Creating a Positive Feedback Loop:** Discovering how acknowledging and celebrating small triumphs can create a positive feedback loop of motivation and progress.

6. **The Role of Gratitude:** Embracing the practice of gratitude and how it can amplify your appreciation for life's smaller joys and victories.

As you journey through these pages, immerse yourself in the empowering task of recognizing and celebrating the smaller triumphs in life. Let this chapter be a reminder that every step, no matter how small, brings you closer to your goals and contributes to your overall sense of fulfillment.

Your life is a tapestry woven with countless small triumphs, and by acknowledging and celebrating them, you can find joy and satisfaction in the journey itself. So, dear reader, **read with a sense of appreciation for life's smaller moments of triumph, for they are the building blocks of your larger successes and a testament to your resilience and determination.**

• **Reflect on your own challenges that seem smaller and how you can emerge stronger.**

Challenges come in many forms, and while some may appear smaller or less daunting than others, each challenge carries within it the potential for growth, learning, and resilience. In this chapter, we will delve deep into the significance of reflecting on the challenges in your life, especially those that may seem minor or less significant. These challenges, despite their size, have the power to help you emerge stronger and more resilient on your journey through life.

As you embark on this chapter, take a moment to consider the challenges you have faced and continue to encounter. Some may have felt like monumental obstacles, while others may have seemed like mere bumps in the road. However, it is crucial to understand that the size or scale of a challenge does not determine its impact on your personal growth and development.

Challenges, regardless of their perceived magnitude, provide opportunities for self-discovery, adaptation, and personal growth. They are the crucibles in which your character is forged, and they hold valuable lessons that can shape your future actions and decisions. This chapter invites you to explore the art of reflection, allowing you to glean insights and wisdom from the challenges, no matter how small they may seem.

Throughout this chapter, we will delve into several key areas:

1. **The Nature of Challenges:** Challenges are an inevitable part of life's journey. They vary in form, size, and intensity, but each one carries its unique set of lessons and opportunities for growth.

2. **Perception and Perspective:** Your perception and perspective play a significant role in how you approach and navigate challenges. Shifting your viewpoint can lead to different outcomes and lessons.

3. **The Power of Self-Reflection:** Self-reflection is a powerful tool for gaining insights into your experiences. It allows you to examine your reactions, emotions, and actions in the face of challenges.

4. **Identifying Growth Opportunities:** Even seemingly smaller challenges offer opportunities for personal growth, resilience, and self-improvement. We will explore how to recognize these opportunities.

5. **Building Problem-Solving Skills:** Challenges, regardless of their size, can enhance your problem-solving skills and adaptability. We will discuss how you can develop these skills through your experiences.

6. **Applying Lessons Learned:** The lessons and insights gained from smaller challenges can be applied to tackle more significant obstacles in the future. We will explore practical ways to integrate these lessons into your life.

As you read these pages, immerse yourself in the empowering process of reflection. Take the time to consider the challenges you have faced, both small and large, and how they have contributed to your personal growth and resilience. Embrace the idea that even the seemingly minor challenges have played a significant role in shaping the resilient and capable individual you are today.

Your journey is a tapestry woven with threads of challenges, and each one has contributed to the unique pattern of your life. By reflecting on these challenges, you can uncover the wisdom and strength that reside within you, allowing you to navigate the complexities of life with greater confidence and resilience.

So, dear reader, **approach this chapter with an open heart and a willingness to explore the lessons hidden within your own challenges, for they are the steppingstones on your path to personal growth and self-discovery.**

- **Share stories of resilience with smaller challenges in life with friends who might need a dose of inspiration.**

Life is a journey filled with both grand adventures and smaller, everyday challenges. While the monumental achievements often grab our attention, it's the stories of resilience in the face of smaller challenges that can be equally inspiring and transformative. In this chapter, we will explore the power of sharing these stories of resilience with friends and loved ones who may benefit from a dose of inspiration.

Think about it – throughout your life, you have encountered a myriad of challenges, some of which may have seemed inconsequential at the time. These challenges may not have garnered headlines or applause, but they were moments where you demonstrated strength, perseverance, and resilience. These are the stories that hold immense power, for they highlight the indomitable spirit of the human experience.

This chapter invites you to reflect on these moments and consider the impact they can have when shared with friends and loved ones facing their challenges. By sharing stories of resilience in the face of smaller challenges, you become a source of inspiration and support for those around you. Your experiences serve as a reminder that resilience is a skill that can be cultivated and that even the smallest victories are worth celebrating.

Throughout this chapter, we will delve into several key areas:

1. **The Resilience in Everyday Challenges:** Recognizing that resilience isn't limited to overcoming major obstacles. It is equally present in the everyday challenges we encounter.

2. **The Power of Storytelling:** Exploring how storytelling is a powerful tool for conveying experiences and lessons. Stories have the ability to inspire and connect with others on a deep level.

3. **Sharing Your Own Experiences:** Reflecting on your own experiences of resilience in the face of smaller challenges and how they have shaped you.

4. **Becoming a Source of Inspiration:** Understanding how sharing your stories can offer inspiration, encouragement, and support to friends and loved ones who may be facing their challenges.

5. **The Ripple Effect of Resilience:** Recognizing that your acts of resilience and the stories you share can create a ripple effect, inspiring others to face their challenges with courage and determination.

6. **Empathy and Connection:** Exploring how sharing stories of resilience fosters empathy and a sense of connection among friends and loved ones.

As you journey through these pages, embrace the idea that your experiences, no matter how small they may seem, carry valuable lessons and insights that can benefit others. Allow yourself to become a storyteller, sharing your moments of resilience with those who may need a reminder of their own inner strength.

Your life is a tapestry woven with threads of resilience, and by sharing these stories, you become a weaver of inspiration and hope. Your willingness to open up and share your experiences can create a sense of community and support, reminding everyone that they, too, possess the resilience to face life's challenges.

So, dear reader, **approach this chapter with the intention of becoming a beacon of inspiration for your friends and loved ones. Your stories of resilience have the power to uplift, motivate, and empower others on their own journeys.**

~ ~ ~ ~ ~ ~

" "Before we dive into Chapter 5, let's get ready for an exciting journey of More Action Over Reflection.
If you do not already have one, grab a piece of paper and write 'Bucket List' at the top.
Now, start jotting down all the things, big or small, that have crossed your mind as something you have wanted to do or thought about doing.
This list can encompass dreams you have never thought you could afford, as well as the tiniest aspirations.
This book is not 'one size fits all'; nor one that tells you to get your finances in order, eat better, or whatever you personally wish to make better in your life.
That comes from what you write down and act upon after you finish reading this book."

~ ~ ~ ~ ~ ~

YOUR
PERSONAL
GROWTH
TOOLBOX

Chapter 5: Your Personal Growth Toolbox

- **Embrace what you have written along with practical tools and tips for self-improvement with enthusiasm.**

In this chapter, we dive deep into the art of embracing your written words, your thoughts, and your journey towards self-improvement with unwavering enthusiasm. It is a journey that starts with reflection and culminates in practical tools and tips that empower you to become the best version of yourself.

As you embark on this chapter, envision it as a personal conversation between you and the potential for growth that lies within your own words. Your written thoughts, whether they are journal entries, personal essays, or simply notes to yourself, hold a wealth of wisdom and self-awareness. They are a mirror reflecting your innermost desires, aspirations, and challenges.

The Power of Reflection

Reflection is a powerful tool for personal growth. It allows you to gain clarity on your goals, understand your values, and identify areas where you want to improve. When you embrace what you have written, you are essentially opening the door to self-discovery.

Take a moment to ponder the questions your own words may raise. What patterns do you notice in your thoughts and emotions? Are there recurring themes or goals that you have expressed in your writing? By reflecting on your own written words, you can gain valuable insights into your own psyche.

From Reflection to Action

However, self-improvement is not solely about introspection; it is about taking action. Your enthusiasm for growth is the driving force that propels you from reflection to action. It is the spark that ignites change and transformation.

Now, let us explore some practical tools and tips for self-improvement that you can embrace with enthusiasm:

1. **Goal Setting:** Your written words often contain aspirations and dreams. Use them as a foundation for setting clear and achievable goals. Whether it is improving your health, advancing your career, or cultivating meaningful relationships, your written thoughts can guide your goal-setting process.

2. **Planning and Organization:** Enthusiasm for self-improvement is bolstered by effective planning and organization. Break down your goals into actionable steps, create a timeline, and establish a system for tracking your progress. Your written words can serve as your roadmap.

3. **Mindfulness and Self-Awareness:** Cultivate mindfulness by regularly revisiting your written thoughts. Practice self-awareness by acknowledging your strengths and areas for growth. Embrace mindfulness techniques like meditation or journaling to deepen your self-awareness.

4. **Continuous Learning:** Enthusiasm for self-improvement often includes a thirst for knowledge. Explore subjects that align with your interests and goals. Whether it is reading books, taking courses, or seeking mentors, continuous learning is a pathway to growth.

5. **Healthy Habits:** Your written words may reveal areas where you want to improve your habits. Whether it is fitness, nutrition, or sleep hygiene, embrace healthy habits that support your well-being. Start small, and gradually build sustainable routines.

6. **Resilience and Adaptability:** Challenges are a natural part of the self-improvement journey. Embrace them with resilience and adaptability. Your written reflections can remind you of past challenges you have overcome, serving as a source of strength.

7. **Accountability:** Share your self-improvement goals and progress with trusted friends or a mentor. Accountability can fuel your enthusiasm and help you stay on track.

8. **Celebrate Progress:** Embrace the habit of celebrating your achievements, no matter how small. Your written words can serve as a record of your progress and successes.

9. **Self-Compassion:** Remember to be kind to yourself along the journey. Embrace self-compassion as a vital component of self-improvement. Your written thoughts can remind you of your inherent worth and value.

The Role of Enthusiasm

Enthusiasm is the driving force that propels you forward on your self-improvement journey. It is the passion that infuses your actions with energy and purpose. As you embrace what you have written and the practical tools for self-improvement, let enthusiasm be your constant companion.

Enthusiasm is infectious; it inspires those around you and draws them into your journey. Share your enthusiasm with friends and loved ones and encourage them to embark on their paths of self-improvement. Your enthusiasm can create a ripple effect of positive change in your community.

In this chapter, you are not alone in your quest for self-improvement. Your written words are your guides, and enthusiasm is your driving force. Embrace the journey with open arms, knowing that every step you take brings you closer to the best version of yourself.

So, dear reader, **as you immerse yourself in this chapter, do so with enthusiasm and a deep sense of purpose. Your enthusiasm is the key that unlocks the doors to personal growth and transformation. Embrace your written words and let them light the way towards a brighter and more fulfilled future.**

• **Set achievable, personal goals, and do not forget to celebrate the small victories.**

In this section, we embark on a journey of setting achievable, personal goals and celebrating the small victories along the way. It is a section dedicated to the art of intentional growth and the joy of progress. As you delve into this section, envision it as your roadmap to personal achievement and fulfillment.

The Power of Goal Setting

Setting goals is a fundamental aspect of personal growth and development. Goals provide direction, motivation, and a sense of purpose. They give you a clear target to aim for and create a framework for making decisions and taking action.

However, not all goals are created equal. In this section, we will explore the art of setting achievable, personal goals. These are goals that resonate with your values, align with your unique aspirations, and are within your reach. They are the steppingstones that lead you towards your larger vision for a more fulfilling life.

The Three Ps of Achievable Goals

Achievable goals are characterized by the Three Ps: Personal, Practical, and Purposeful.

1. **Personal:** Achievable goals are deeply personal. They reflect your individual desires, passions, and priorities. They are not imposed by external expectations or societal pressures. In this section, you will reflect on how to identify and articulate your personal goals, ones that truly matter to you.

2. **Practical:** Achievable goals are practical and realistic. They take into account your current resources, constraints, and circumstances. You will discover how to set goals that are attainable within your existing framework, whether it is related to time, finances, or other resources.

3. **Purposeful:** Achievable goals are purposeful and meaningful. They connect to your larger life purpose and values. You will explore how to align your goals with what

truly matters to you, ensuring that each goal you pursue brings a sense of fulfillment.

The Process of Goal Setting

Setting achievable, personal goals involves a deliberate process:

1. **Reflection:** Begin by reflecting on your values, passions, and long-term aspirations. What matters most to you in life? What are your core values? What do you envision for your future? This introspective phase helps you identify what truly resonates with you.

2. **Clarity:** Define your goals with clarity. Use the SMART criteria—**Specific, Measurable, Achievable, Relevant, and Time-bound**—to articulate your goals in a way that makes them tangible and actionable.

3. **Prioritization:** Prioritize your goals based on their significance and impact on your life. Not all goals need to be pursued simultaneously. This section guides you in selecting the most important ones to focus on.

4. **Action Planning:** Develop action plans for each goal. Break them down into smaller, manageable steps. Determine the resources, skills, and support needed to achieve them.

5. **Monitoring and Adjusting:** Regularly monitor your progress towards your goals. Celebrate small victories along the way. If necessary, adjust your goals or action plans based on your evolving circumstances and insights.

The Joy of Celebrating Small Victories

Celebrating small victories is a vital aspect of goal achievement. It is a practice that infuses your journey with motivation and positivity. In this section, you will explore the importance of acknowledging and celebrating your progress, no matter how incremental it may seem.

Small victories serve several essential purposes:

1. **Motivation:** Celebrating small wins provides a boost of motivation. It reinforces your belief in your ability to achieve larger goals. It is a reminder that you are making progress.

2. **Positive Reinforcement:** Positive emotions associated with celebrating victories create a positive feedback loop. When you feel good about your achievements, you are more likely to continue taking action towards your goals.

3. **Reflection:** Celebrating small victories allows you to reflect on your journey. It is an opportunity to acknowledge the effort, perseverance, and growth that have taken place.

4. **Gratitude:** Small victories encourage gratitude. They remind you of the resources, support, and opportunities that have contributed to your progress.

The Journey of Personal Growth

As you navigate the process of setting achievable, personal goals and celebrating small victories, remember that personal growth is a journey, not a destination. Your goals are the milestones that mark your path, and each victory is a step forward.

In this section, you are not alone on your journey. You have the guidance and insights needed to set meaningful goals that align with your values and celebrate your progress. Your goals are unique to you, reflecting your passions, dreams, and aspirations.

So, dear reader, as you immerse yourself in this section, embrace the power of setting achievable, personal goals and relish the joy of celebrating the small victories along the way. Your journey of personal growth is a testament to your commitment to living a fulfilling and purposeful life. **May each goal you set and every small victory you celebrate bring you closer to the life you envision for yourself.**

• Share your journey and insights with friends who are also on a path of self-discovery.

In this section, we delve into the profound journey of self-discovery. It is a section dedicated to the exploration of your inner self, the unveiling of your true potential, and the realization of your authentic identity. As you immerse yourself in the pages ahead, envision it as a voyage into the depths of your being, a journey that holds the promise of self-awareness and personal transformation.

The Quest for Self-Discovery

Self-discovery is a fundamental aspect of personal growth and development. It involves gaining insight into your thoughts, emotions, desires, and beliefs. It is the process of uncovering your values, passions, and purpose in life. Self-discovery is akin to embarking on a quest to understand the essence of who you truly are.

However, the path of self-discovery is not always straightforward. It may require introspection, reflection, and a willingness to confront both the light and shadow aspects of your psyche. Yet, the rewards of self-discovery are immeasurable. It leads to greater self-acceptance, improved decision-making, enhanced relationships, and a deeper sense of fulfillment.

The Layers of Self

As you begin your journey of self-discovery, consider that the self is not a singular entity but a complex interplay of various layers. These layers include:

1. **The Surface Self:** This is the aspect of your identity that is readily visible to others. It includes your external roles, such as your profession, hobbies, and social status.

2. **The Ego Self:** The ego is the conscious part of your identity that you associate with your individuality. It encompasses your thoughts, feelings, and beliefs about yourself.

3. **The Authentic Self:** At the core of your being lies your authentic self. This is the part of you that is genuine, unaffected by societal expectations or external influences. It represents your true essence, values, and purpose.

4. **The Shadow Self:** The shadow self consists of aspects of your personality that you may suppress or deny. These can include fears, insecurities, and unresolved emotions. Exploring the shadow self is a crucial aspect of self-discovery.

The Process of Self-Discovery

Self-discovery is an ongoing and dynamic process. It involves a series of steps and practices that lead to greater self-awareness. Here is a brief overview of the process:

1. **Reflection:** Begin by setting aside time for introspection and reflection. Ask yourself profound questions about your life, values, passions, and dreams. Journaling can be a valuable tool in this phase.

2. **Mindfulness:** Cultivate mindfulness, the practice of being fully present in the moment. Mindfulness allows you to observe your thoughts, emotions, and sensations without judgment, leading to greater self-awareness.

3. **Exploration:** Explore your interests and passions. Engage in activities that bring you joy and fulfillment. Your passions often provide clues to your authentic self.

4. **Confronting the Shadow:** Acknowledge and explore the shadow aspects of your personality. This may involve facing fears, healing past wounds, and embracing your vulnerabilities.

5. **Seeking Feedback:** Seek feedback from trusted friends, mentors, or therapists. They can offer valuable insights into your strengths and areas for growth.

6. **Embracing Vulnerability:** Embrace vulnerability as a pathway to authenticity. Vulnerability involves showing your true self, imperfections, and all, to others.

The Gifts of Self-Discovery

Self-discovery yields numerous gifts, each contributing to your personal growth and well-being:

1. **Self-Acceptance:** Self-discovery fosters self-acceptance, allowing you to embrace your strengths and imperfections with compassion.

2. **Improved Relationships:** Understanding yourself better enables you to connect more authentically with others and cultivate healthier relationships.

3. **Clarity of Purpose:** Self-discovery unveils your values and passions, helping you clarify your life's purpose and direction.

4. **Enhanced Decision-Making:** Greater self-awareness empowers you to make decisions that align with your authentic self.

5. **Resilience:** Self-discovery equips you with emotional resilience, enabling you to navigate life's challenges with grace.

Sharing Your Journey

As you embark on your journey of self-discovery, consider the profound impact it can have on your life. It is not just a solitary quest; it is an opportunity to share your insights, wisdom, and experiences with friends who are also on a path of self-discovery.

Sharing your journey can take various forms:

1. **Conversations:** Engage in open and honest conversations with friends about your self-discovery journey. Share your challenges, breakthroughs, and realizations.

2. **Support:** Offer support and encouragement to friends who are also exploring their authentic selves. Be a source of inspiration and motivation for one another.

3. **Group Exploration:** Consider forming or joining a self-discovery group with friends. These groups provide a space for collective growth and shared learning.

4. **Collaboration:** Collaborate on projects or activities that align with your shared values and passions. Your combined efforts can lead to meaningful contributions to your communities or causes you care about.

5. **Reflect Together:** Reflect together on your individual and collective journeys. Discuss how self-discovery has influenced your lives and the positive changes it has brought.

The Continuation of Your Journey

As you delve into the depths of self-discovery and share your insights with friends, remember that the journey is ongoing. Self-discovery is not a destination but a lifelong exploration. Embrace the process with curiosity, compassion, and an open heart.

Your journey of self-discovery is a testament to your commitment to living an authentic and fulfilling life. It is an exploration of your inner landscape, a journey into the core of your being. **May it lead you to profound self-awareness, deep connections with others, and a life that resonates with purpose and authenticity.**

Chapter 6: Embrace Diversity and Unity

• Continue Your Actions and Celebrate the Tapestry of Differences

In this final chapter, we embark on a journey of action and celebration. It is a chapter that invites you to put into practice the insights and wisdom you have gained throughout this book. It is also a chapter that celebrates the rich tapestry of differences that define our lives, reminding us of the beauty that emerges from diversity and unity.

Taking Action: Your Journey's Next Steps

Throughout this book, you have explored various aspects of life, from embracing your age with confidence to finding joy in everyday moments, conquering life's challenges, fostering unity and inclusivity, and embarking on a journey of self-discovery. These insights are not meant to remain words on pages but to be transformed into actions that enrich your life and the lives of those around you.

Action is the catalyst for change and growth. It is the bridge between intention and realization. As you continue your journey, remember that every small step you take has the potential to create ripples of positive impact. Here are some key actions to consider:

1. **Embrace Your Age with Confidence:** Put into practice the confidence-building strategies discussed in Chapter 1. Embrace your age proudly and inspire others to do the same.

2. **Find Joy in Everyday Moments:** Actively seek out moments of joy in your daily life. Savor them, share them, and let them fill your heart with gratitude.

3. **Conquer Life's Challenges:** When faced with new challenges, apply the resilience strategies from Chapters 3

and 4. Approach obstacles with determination, knowing that you have the strength to overcome them.

4. **Foster Unity and Inclusivity:** Actively engage in building a sense of community and inclusivity in your life. Reach out to people from diverse backgrounds and celebrate the beauty of differences.

5. **Share Your Journey and Insights:** Act on the insights gained from your journey of self-discovery, as explored in Chapter 5. Share your wisdom and experiences with others who are on a similar path.

6. **Celebrate Differences:** Embrace and celebrate the differences you encounter in your interactions with people from various walks of life. Recognize that these differences enrich our collective tapestry.

7. **Inspire Positive Change:** Take action to make a meaningful difference in the lives of others. Share your wisdom, lend a helping hand, and be a source of inspiration.

The Beauty of Diversity and Unity

Our world is a kaleidoscope of cultures, beliefs, backgrounds, and perspectives. It is a place where diversity flourishes, offering a wealth of experiences and insights. Diversity is not just a fact; it is a source of immense strength and creativity. It is a reminder that every individual is a unique thread in the grand tapestry of humanity.

In this chapter, we celebrate the beauty of differences. We recognize that our dissimilarities are what make us extraordinary. They challenge our perspectives, broaden our horizons, and inspire innovation. Differences remind us that we are all part of a larger whole, connected by our shared humanity.

Unity is the thread that weaves through the tapestry of diversity. It is the understanding that despite our differences, we are all part of the same human family. Unity does not require conformity; it thrives on acceptance and respect. It is the acknowledgment that every individual, regardless of their background, has inherent worth and dignity.

As you celebrate the tapestry of differences in your life, consider the following:

1. **Learn from Differences:** Embrace the opportunity to learn from people with diverse backgrounds. Engage in conversations that challenge your assumptions and broaden your understanding.

2. **Empathy and Compassion:** Cultivate empathy and compassion for others. Understand that each person carries their own burdens and joys, and your kindness can make a significant difference.

3. **Break Down Barriers:** Actively work to break down barriers that divide us. Advocate for inclusivity and equality in your community and society.

4. **Foster Dialogue:** Encourage open and respectful dialogue among people with differing viewpoints. It is through conversation that understanding and common ground can be found.

5. **Celebrate Achievements:** Celebrate the achievements and contributions of individuals from all backgrounds. Recognize that diversity enhances creativity and innovation.

6. **Promote Equal Opportunities:** Advocate for equal opportunities for all, regardless of their race, gender, age, or

other characteristics. Support organizations and initiatives that promote diversity and inclusion.

7. **Lead by Example:** Lead by example in embracing and celebrating differences. Your actions can inspire others to do the same.

Your Ongoing Journey

As you take action and celebrate the tapestry of differences, remember that your journey is a continuous one. Life is a series of interconnected chapters, each offering new opportunities for growth and transformation. Embrace each moment with enthusiasm and an open heart.

Your journey is a testament to your commitment to personal growth, self-awareness, and positive change. It is a reflection of your desire to live a life filled with purpose, authenticity, and compassion. As you continue your journey, may you find fulfillment in every step you take and may your actions create a ripple effect of positivity in the world.

In this book, every word, every thought, and every page has been dedicated to you, dear reader. Your life is a masterpiece in progress, and together, we have celebrated, learned, and grown. Now, as you continue your journey, know that the boundless potential of age and the beauty of differences are yours to explore and embrace.

So, dear reader, continue your actions, celebrate the tapestry of differences, and may your life be a testament to the transformative power of embracing every moment with love, wisdom, and boundless potential.

• **Share your thoughts on your personal life changes, as well as the inclusive message of your life with friends.**

In this final chapter, we explore the importance of sharing your thoughts on your personal life changes and the inclusive message of your life with friends. Your journey has been a remarkable tapestry of experiences, growth, and inclusivity, and now is the time to reflect upon these changes and communicate them with those you care about.

Reflecting on Personal Life Changes

Your life is an ever-evolving journey, marked by significant personal changes and transformations. As you reflect on these changes, consider the following aspects:

1. **Life Milestones:** Think about the significant milestones you have reached. These could include career achievements, personal goals, or important life events like marriage, parenthood, or retirement.

2. **Challenges Overcome:** Reflect on the challenges you have faced and conquered. These experiences have shaped your resilience and character. They serve as powerful reminders of your inner strength.

3. **Personal Growth:** Consider how you have grown as an individual. Your journey may have led you to discover new passions, skills, or talents. Reflect on the ways in which you have evolved and developed.

4. **Changing Perspectives:** Think about how your perspectives and beliefs have evolved over time. Are there particular experiences or moments that have influenced your outlook on life, relationships, or the world?

5. **Lifestyle Changes:** Reflect on any lifestyle changes you have made for better health, well-being, or personal fulfillment. Whether it is adopting a healthier diet, starting

a fitness routine, or pursuing new hobbies, these changes are worth acknowledging.

Sharing Your Personal Changes

Once you have reflected on your personal life changes, it is time to share these insights with your friends. Here is how you can do it:

1. **Open Conversations:** Initiate open and honest conversations with your friends. Share the personal changes you have undergone and how they have impacted your life.

2. **Listen Actively:** Encourage your friends to share their own experiences and changes. Actively listen to their stories and offer support and empathy.

3. **Offer Inspiration:** Your personal changes can inspire your friends to embark on their journeys of self-improvement. Share your challenges and successes to motivate them.

4. **Celebrate Achievements:** Celebrate your achievements with your friends. Let them know about your milestones and how they have contributed to your growth and happiness.

5. **Discuss Challenges:** Do not shy away from discussing challenges or setbacks you have encountered. Sharing these moments of vulnerability can foster deeper connections with your friends.

The Inclusive Message of Your Life

Your life journey has also been characterized by inclusivity and a celebration of diversity. Here is how you can share the inclusive message of your life with friends:

1. **Promote Understanding:** Engage your friends in discussions about the importance of inclusivity and acceptance. Share your experiences of embracing diversity and how it has enriched your life.

2. **Challenge Prejudice:** If you encounter instances of prejudice or bias in conversations, kindly challenge them. Share stories and examples that illustrate the value of inclusivity.

3. **Inspire Unity:** Your message of inclusivity can foster unity among your friends. Encourage them to appreciate the unique qualities and backgrounds of one another.

4. **Support Inclusive Actions:** Get involved in activities or initiatives that promote inclusivity and equality. Invite your friends to join you in supporting these causes.

5. **Share Resources:** Recommend books, articles, documentaries, or workshops that highlight the importance of inclusivity. Encourage your friends to educate themselves on these subjects.

The Impact of Sharing

Sharing your thoughts on personal life changes and the inclusive message of your life can have a profound impact:

1. **Deepening Bonds:** Open and honest conversations can strengthen the bonds of friendship. Sharing personal changes and inclusivity messages can create a more supportive and connected friend group.

2. **Mutual Inspiration:** Your personal journey can inspire your friends to embark on their paths of self-improvement.

Likewise, your inclusive message can motivate them to embrace diversity and unity.

3. **Enhancing Perspectives:** Sharing experiences and insights can broaden your friends' perspectives. It can encourage them to approach life with a more inclusive and empathetic mindset.

4. **Promoting Change:** Your conversations may inspire your friends to become advocates for inclusivity and equality. Your message can influence positive change within your community.

5. **Creating a Legacy:** Your legacy is not just about personal achievements; it is also about the positive impact you have on others. Sharing your journey and inclusive message contributes to this legacy.

Continuing the Journey

As you share your thoughts and inclusive message, remember that your journey is ongoing. **Life is a continuous exploration of personal growth,** inclusivity, and understanding. Your openness to change and your commitment to inclusivity are powerful forces that shape the world around you.

• Encouraging your friends to read and discuss their life changes is a powerful way to foster unity, understanding, and personal growth within your social circle.

This section dives deep into the significance of promoting open and meaningful dialogues among friends about the various transformations and milestones that shape their lives. It is about creating an environment where everyone feels valued and supported in sharing their unique journeys, and it goes beyond mere conversation—it is a journey of self-discovery and mutual inspiration.

Reflecting on Life Changes

Life is an ever-evolving journey, marked by a series of changes, both big and small. Each person's path is filled with milestones, challenges, and growth opportunities. As you embark on the mission of encouraging your friends to reflect on their life changes, consider the following aspects:

1. **Acknowledge Milestones:** Begin by acknowledging the significant milestones your friends have achieved. These could include career advancements, personal goals accomplished, or life events such as marriage, parenthood, or relocating to a new place. Recognizing these milestones is a way of celebrating their achievements.

2. **Challenges Overcome:** Encourage your friends to reflect on the challenges they have encountered and successfully overcome. Life is full of obstacles, and sharing stories of resilience can inspire others who may be facing similar difficulties.

3. **Personal Growth:** Emphasize personal growth as a fundamental part of everyone's journey. Ask your friends to consider how they have evolved as individuals over time.

Have they discovered new interests, talents, or passions along the way? Self-discovery is a transformative process worth exploring.

4. **Changing Perspectives:** Invite your friends to reflect on how their perspectives and beliefs have evolved. Life experiences can profoundly influence one's outlook on life, relationships, and the world. Encourage them to share moments or events that have shaped their current perspectives.

5. **Lifestyle Changes:** Explore any lifestyle changes your friends have embraced to improve their well-being and overall fulfillment. Whether it is adopting a healthier diet, starting an exercise routine, or pursuing new hobbies, these changes contribute to personal growth and should be acknowledged.

Initiating Open Conversations

Once your friends have taken time to reflect on their life changes, it is time to initiate open and meaningful conversations. Here is how you can encourage these dialogues:

1. **Create a Safe Space:** Ensure that the environment is welcoming and non-judgmental. Everyone should feel comfortable sharing their experiences and thoughts without fear of criticism.

2. **Listen Actively:** Encourage active listening during these conversations. It is important for friends to listen attentively to each other's stories, offering empathy and support.

3. **Share Personal Experiences:** Lead by example by sharing your own life changes and experiences. This can set the tone for open and honest sharing within the group.

4. **Celebrate Achievements:** Celebrate each other's milestones and achievements. Offer congratulations and support for the goals that have been reached.

5. **Discuss Challenges:** Do not shy away from discussing challenges or setbacks. They are an integral part of life and can provide valuable learning experiences. Sharing these moments of vulnerability can foster deeper connections.

Fostering Unity and Understanding

Encouraging your friends to read and discuss their life changes has the power to foster unity and understanding within your group. Here is how:

1. **Strengthening Bonds:** Open and honest conversations deepen the bonds of friendship. When friends share their life changes and experiences, it creates a more supportive and connected group.

2. **Mutual Inspiration:** Each person's journey can inspire others within the group to pursue their own paths of self-improvement. Hearing about your friends' achievements can motivate others to set and achieve their goals.

3. **Expanding Perspectives:** Sharing experiences and insights broadens everyone's perspectives. It encourages friends to approach life with greater empathy and a more inclusive mindset.

4. **Advocating for Change:** These conversations may inspire your friends to become advocates for change, both individually and collectively. They may be motivated to address specific issues or contribute positively to their communities.

5. **Creating Lasting Bonds:** By fostering unity and understanding, you create lasting bonds among your friends. These connections can provide ongoing support and encouragement throughout life's journey.

Continuing the Journey

Encouraging your friends to read and discuss their life changes is a valuable endeavor that promotes unity and understanding within your social circle. It is an opportunity to celebrate achievements, share challenges, and inspire one another. By creating an open and supportive environment, you contribute to the growth and well-being of your friends and strengthen the bonds of friendship that will endure over time. **This journey of self-discovery and mutual inspiration is a testament to the power of genuine connection and meaningful conversation.**

~ ~ ~ ~ ~ ~ ~ ~ ~ ~ ~

Epilogue:
• Take a moment to reflect on your personal journey through this book and through your life and jot down your thoughts.

As you reach the final pages of this book, it is an opportune moment to pause and reflect on the incredible journey you have embarked upon. Throughout the chapters, we have explored various aspects of life, personal growth, and the power of human connection. Your personal journey through this book is a reflection of your own unique life journey, and it is worth taking some time to gather your thoughts and jot down your additional reflections.

Reflecting on Your Personal Journey

Your journey through this book mirrors the journey of life itself. Each chapter has offered insights, wisdom, and guidance on different aspects of life, from embracing your age with confidence to finding joy in everyday moments, conquering life's challenges, fostering inclusivity, and sharing your story with others. As you reflect on your personal journey through this book, consider the following points:

1. **Highlights and Insights:** Think about the chapters or sections that resonated with you the most. Were there particular insights that stood out? Moments of inspiration that left a lasting impact. Jot down these highlights and what they meant to you.

2. **Personal Growth:** Consider how your perspective may have evolved as you journeyed through the pages. Have you gained a deeper understanding of yourself or the world around you? Reflect on the ways in which this book has contributed to your personal growth.

3. **Application in Life:** Take a moment to think about how you can apply the principles and lessons from this book to your everyday life. Are there specific actions or changes you would like to implement based on what you have learned?

4. **Connections to Your Journey:** Explore the connections between the book's content and your own life journey. Are there parallels between the advice offered in these pages and your own experiences? How can these connections guide you in your path forward?

5. **Impact on Others:** Consider how the knowledge and insights gained from this book can positively impact the

lives of those around you. Are there friends, family members, or colleagues who might benefit from the wisdom you have acquired?

Jotting Down Your Additional Thoughts

Now that you have taken a moment to reflect on your personal journey through this book, it is time to jot down your additional thoughts. Grab a notebook, journal, or a blank page and let your thoughts flow. Here are some prompts to help you get started:

1. **Gratitude:** Express gratitude for the opportunity to explore these valuable insights. What are you grateful for as you reach the end of this journey?

2. **Personal Insights:** Share any personal insights or "aha" moments you have had while reading this book. What new perspectives have you gained?

3. **Goals and Intentions:** Consider any goals or intentions you have set for yourself based on the book's content. How do you plan to integrate these changes into your life?

4. **Action Steps:** Outline specific action steps you would like to take moving forward. How can you apply the principles discussed in the book to create a more fulfilling and meaningful life?

5. **Sharing with Others:** Think about how you can share the knowledge and wisdom you have gained with friends, family, or colleagues. How might you inspire positive change in their lives?

6. **Life's Journey:** Reflect on the concept of life as a journey. What are your thoughts on the idea that every moment,

challenge, and experience contributes to the tapestry of your life?

7. **Final Words:** If you were to offer a few final words of wisdom or encouragement to fellow readers or friends, what would you say?

Continuing Your Journey

As you jot down your additional thoughts and reflections, remember that your journey is an ongoing and ever-evolving process. Life is a continuous exploration of self-discovery, personal growth, and connection with others. The insights and lessons you have gained from this book are valuable tools that can accompany you on your path forward.

Whether you choose to revisit these pages in the future, share your newfound wisdom with others, or simply continue your journey with an open heart and mind, know that the journey itself is a remarkable and transformative experience. Each step you take, each reflection you make, and each connection you foster adds to the rich tapestry of your life.

In closing, embrace the wisdom you have gained, celebrate the beauty of your unique journey, and carry forward the boundless potential of age with confidence and purpose. **Your story is a masterpiece in progress, and every moment is an opportunity to create a life filled with love, wisdom, and positive impact.**

• This book is your companion, not a rulebook. It is here to applaud your life and guide you towards a better self.

A Companion on Your Unique Journey

Imagine this book as a trusted companion on your life's journey, walking alongside you, celebrating your achievements, and offering guidance when needed. It is not a rulebook filled with rigid instructions; instead, it is a source of inspiration and support tailored to your individual experiences.

Applauding Your Life

Life is a grand tapestry woven with moments of joy, challenges, victories, and growth. This book applauds your life in all its uniqueness. It acknowledges that your journey is unlike any other, and every twist and turn in your path has shaped you into the remarkable person you are today.

Within these pages, you will find celebrations of your milestones, big and small. Whether it is a personal achievement, a moment of clarity, or a simple act of kindness, this book applauds your efforts and reminds you of the significance of these moments in your life.

Guidance Toward Self-Improvement

While celebrating your life, this book also gently guides you toward becoming a better version of yourself. It recognizes that personal growth is a continuous journey, and it offers insights and wisdom to support your development.

Rather than imposing rigid rules, this book encourages self-reflection and self-awareness. It invites you to explore your values, passions, and aspirations. It provides tools and ideas to help you set meaningful goals and take steps toward achieving them.

Embracing Positivity

One of the key aspects of this book is its emphasis on positivity. It encourages you to focus on the brighter side of life, to find joy in everyday moments, and to cultivate a mindset that promotes happiness and well-being.

Throughout the chapters, you have encountered your stories of resilience, examples of kindness, and practical tips for fostering positivity. These elements are woven into the narrative to inspire you to embrace a more positive and optimistic outlook on life.

A Source of Inspiration

As your companion, this book also serves as a wellspring of inspiration. It helped your friends share stories of how they have overcome adversity, pursued their passions, and made a positive impact on the world. These stories are meant to ignite your own sense of purpose and motivation.

Whether you are seeking guidance in your career, relationships, personal development, or simply a dose of inspiration to brighten your day, this book aims to provide the insights and encouragement you need to take meaningful steps forward.

A Journey of Self-Discovery

Ultimately, this book is an invitation to embark on a journey of self-discovery. It recognizes that life's purpose is not a one-size-fits-all concept but rather a deeply personal exploration of what brings meaning and fulfillment to your existence.

It encourages you to delve into your own values, passions, and beliefs. It invites you to question, reflect, and seek answers within yourself. Through this process of self-discovery, you uncovered your unique path and defined what a "better self" means to you.

The Boundless Potential of Age

Age is not a limitation but a source of boundless potential. Whether you are in your 70s,80s,90s, or beyond, this book reminds you that every stage of life is an opportunity for growth, learning, and transformation.

It celebrates the wisdom and experience that come with age and encourages you to embrace the richness of each life stage. It is a reminder that there are no expiration dates on dreams, goals, or aspirations.

Your Personal Journey

In closing, this book is not just a collection of words on pages; it is a living companion on your personal journey. It applauds your life, offers guidance for self-improvement, and inspires you to embrace the boundless potential of age.

As you turned each page, remember that your journey is unique, your experiences are valuable, and your potential for growth is limitless. Let this book be your steadfast companion, walking beside you as you navigate the extraordinary adventure of life.

• Share your reflections and experiences with friends, inviting them to join you on this wonderful journey.

The Power of Sharing

Sharing is a profound act that extends beyond the mere exchange of words or experiences. It is a bridge that connects individuals, creating bonds of understanding, empathy, and support. When you choose to share your reflections, experiences, and the wisdom contained within this book with your friends, you open the door to a transformative journey for both you and those you invite to join.

Reflecting Together

Reflection is a powerful tool for personal growth and self-discovery. It allows you to pause, look within, and gain insights into your thoughts, feelings, and experiences. As you have read this book and engaged in self-reflection, you embarked on a journey of understanding yourself on a deeper level.

When you extend an invitation to your friends to reflect together, you create a safe and supportive space for open conversations. These dialogues can lead to valuable insights, as friends share their perspectives, experiences, and unique ways of interpreting the book's messages.

Sharing Experiences

Life is a collection of experiences, both big and small, that shape who we are. This book celebrates the diversity of human experiences and encourages you to embrace your own unique journey. When you share your experiences with friends, you invite them to do the same, fostering a sense of connection and camaraderie.

Your experiences may include moments of triumph, personal challenges overcome, and everyday joys savored. By sharing these experiences, you not only celebrate your own journey but also inspire your friends to recognize the significance of their own life experiences.

Inviting Dialogue

A book is not just a solitary reading experience; it can become a catalyst for meaningful conversations. As you engage with the content of this book and reflect on its messages, you will likely have thoughts, questions, and insights that you would like to discuss.

Inviting your friends to join you in these discussions creates a sense of community and shared learning. You can explore the book's themes, delve into your personal takeaways, and gain new perspectives through the diverse viewpoints of your friends.

Deepening Connections

Sharing your reflections and experiences with friends can deepen your connections on multiple levels. It fosters trust, vulnerability, and a sense of mutual support. It allows you to see your friends in new lights as they share their own journeys and insights.

These deeper connections can lead to stronger friendships, as you discover commonalities, values, and aspirations. It creates a network of individuals who are not only there for each other but also actively engaged in personal growth and self-improvement.

Inspiring Growth

One of the beautiful aspects of sharing is its potential to inspire growth in others. As you discuss the book's messages, your reflections, and your personal experiences, you may find that your friends are inspired to embark on their own journeys of self-discovery and improvement.

Your willingness to share your own challenges and triumphs can motivate and encourage your friends to set their own goals, pursue their passions, and seek greater fulfillment in life. It is a ripple effect of positivity and personal growth.

Strengthening the Support System

Life's journey is filled with ups and downs, and having a strong support system can make all the difference. By inviting your friends to share in this journey, you reinforce the bonds of your support network.

You become not only friends who share hobbies or interests but also companions in the quest for personal development and a more meaningful life. This strengthened support system can provide encouragement during tough times and amplify the joy during moments of celebration.

Embracing Diversity

As you share this book and your experiences with friends, you celebrate the diversity of perspectives and backgrounds that each person brings to the table. It is an acknowledgment that every individual's journey is unique, shaped by their own set of circumstances and choices.

This diversity enriches the collective experience, as friends from different walks of life contribute their own insights and interpretations. It encourages openness, tolerance, and a broader understanding of the world.

The Invitation

So, dear reader, consider this an invitation—a heartfelt call to share your reflections, experiences, and this book with friends. Invite them to join you on this wonderful journey of self-discovery, growth, and mutual support.

Whether you gather for thoughtful discussions, engage in shared activities inspired by the book, or simply exchange thoughts and reflections, know that you are fostering a sense of connection and unity. You are embarking on a collective adventure toward becoming the best versions of yourselves.

Together, you and your friends can celebrate life's milestones, navigate its challenges, savor its joys, and uncover its profound lessons. In this shared journey, you will find not only personal growth but also the beauty of human connections that transcend the pages of a book and transform into a tapestry of shared experiences.

~ ~ ~ ~ ~ ~ ~ ~ ~ ~

Final Thoughts:

- **Share your growth stories casually; they might inspire others.**

The Power of Casual Sharing

Casual sharing is a simple yet profound act that can have a lasting impact on those around you. It involves opening up about your personal growth journey in an informal and relatable manner. Rather than presenting it as a grand narrative, casual sharing allows you to connect with others on a more human level.

Inspiration Through Authenticity

One of the remarkable aspects of casual sharing is its authenticity. When you share your growth stories in a casual, genuine way, it becomes relatable to others. They see you as a real person, not a distant role model. Your authenticity makes your journey accessible and, therefore, more inspiring.

Think about the times when you have been inspired by someone's story. It is often not the polished, larger-than-life narratives that resonate the most. Instead, it is the stories that feel real, relatable, and told in a way that makes you think, "I can do that too."

Breaking Down Barriers

Casual sharing breaks down barriers and creates a sense of connection. It allows you to bridge the gap between your experiences and the experiences of others. **When you share your growth stories informally, it is like having a friendly conversation rather than delivering a formal speech.**

This approach makes it easier for others to relate to your journey, as they do not feel pressured to measure up to unrealistic standards. It encourages a sense of camaraderie and mutual support, fostering an environment where everyone's growth is valued and celebrated.

Small Moments, Big Impact

Growth stories do not always have to be about monumental achievements or life-changing epiphanies. In fact, it is often the small, everyday moments of growth that have the most significant impact. These moments might include:

1. Overcoming a personal fear or limitation.
2. Navigating a challenging situation with resilience.
3. Learning a new skill or hobby.
4. Developing healthier habits.

5. Gaining a deeper understanding of oneself.

When you share these everyday growth stories casually, you highlight the idea that personal development is an ongoing journey filled with both small victories and occasional setbacks. This relatable approach encourages others to embrace their own journeys without feeling overwhelmed by the need for grand achievements.

Fostering a Growth Mindset

Casual sharing also promotes a growth mindset—a belief that abilities and intelligence can be developed through dedication and hard work. When you share your stories of growth, you reinforce the idea that improvement is possible for everyone.

Your willingness to acknowledge the effort and learning involved in your personal development journey can inspire others to adopt a similar mindset. It encourages them to see challenges as opportunities for growth and to persevere in their pursuit of self-improvement.

Creating an Inclusive Environment

Inclusive environments value and celebrate the diversity of experiences and growth journeys. When you casually share your growth stories, you contribute to the creation of such an environment. You send a message that everyone's journey is unique and valid, regardless of its scale or pace.

Inclusivity means recognizing that personal growth is not a one-size-fits-all endeavor. By sharing your experiences in an approachable manner, you invite others to share their stories as well, contributing to a rich tapestry of diverse growth narratives.

Supporting Others

Casual sharing can provide much-needed support to those who may be navigating similar challenges or seeking inspiration. When you share your experiences, you offer guidance, empathy, and encouragement to others who may be at different stages of their journeys.

Your stories can serve as beacons of hope, showing that progress is possible even in the face of obstacles. They remind others that setbacks are part of the growth process, and that perseverance can lead to positive change.

Sparking Conversations

Casual sharing initiates conversations. It encourages dialogues about personal growth, self-improvement, and the strategies and insights gained along the way. These conversations can be enlightening, motivating, and a source of mutual learning.

By sharing your growth stories, you invite others to join in these conversations. You create an atmosphere where individuals feel comfortable discussing their aspirations, challenges, and dreams. In doing so, you contribute to a culture of growth and self-awareness.

Embracing Vulnerability

Casual sharing often involves moments of vulnerability, as you open up about your struggles, setbacks, and moments of self-doubt. Embracing vulnerability is a courageous act that fosters genuine connections with others.

When you share your growth journey, warts, and all, you show that vulnerability is not a sign of weakness but a sign of strength. It is a reminder that growth is a human experience, and no one is exempt from its challenges.

Sharing with Purpose

While casual sharing is informal, it can also be purposeful. Consider the following ways to share your growth stories in a meaningful manner:

1. **Conversations with Friends:** Engage in casual conversations with friends, where you exchange stories of personal growth and encourage one another's journeys.

2. **Social Media:** Share snippets of your growth journey on social media platforms. Use hashtags or captions to connect with others who share similar interests or experiences.

3. **Group Discussions:** Participate in group discussions or forums centered around personal development. Contribute your insights and listen to the experiences of others.

4. **Workshops and Seminars:** If you have expertise in a particular area of personal growth, consider hosting informal workshops or seminars to share your knowledge.

5. **Blogs and Journals:** Start a blog or keep a journal where you document your growth journey. Your written reflections can resonate with others who stumble upon your writings.

6. **Community Engagement:** Get involved in local community events or initiatives that promote personal development and growth. Your presence can inspire those around you.

The Ripple Effect of Inspiration

In conclusion, the act of casually sharing your growth stories is not just about recounting personal achievements; it is about inspiring others to embark on their own journeys of self-discovery and improvement. It is about creating an environment of inclusivity, empathy, and support where everyone's growth is celebrated.

Your stories, whether big or small, become ripples that extend outward, touching the lives of those who hear them. They remind us of all that personal growth is a continuous, shared human experience. So, go ahead and share your growth stories casually, for they have the power to inspire, connect, and uplift those around you on their own journeys of growth and self-realization.

• **Your recommendations can spark positive change in your friends' lives.**

The Influence of Recommendations

Recommendations are more than just suggestions; they are powerful catalysts for change. When you recommend something—a book, a movie, a new hobby, a wellness practice, or even a change in mindset—you are essentially sharing a piece of your own journey and experience. Your recommendations carry the weight of your personal endorsement, making them highly influential.

Fostering Growth and Learning

One of the remarkable aspects of recommendations is their ability to foster growth and learning. When you suggest a book or resource that has had a meaningful impact on your life, you are opening a door to new knowledge and insights for your friends. This act of sharing is a form of continuous learning.

Consider the times when someone recommended a book to you, and it profoundly changed your perspective or provided valuable information. By extending this gift of knowledge to your friends, you empower them to embark on their own journeys of self-improvement and personal growth.

Inspiration Through Example

Your recommendations serve as examples of your values and interests. When you suggest a book that inspired you or a wellness practice that improved your life, you are demonstrating your commitment to personal development and well-being. This leads by example and inspires your friends to explore similar paths.

For instance, if you recommend a meditation app because it has helped you manage stress and find inner peace, you are not just offering a suggestion; you are showing your friends that prioritizing mental well-being is important to you. Your actions can encourage them to explore mindfulness practices and experience their benefits firsthand.

Building Trust and Credibility

Trust is a fundamental component of influence, and your recommendations can strengthen the trust your friends have in your judgment. When you consistently suggest valuable resources or practices, you build credibility as someone who offers reliable guidance.

Think about how you perceive friends or acquaintances who consistently recommend excellent books, provide valuable advice, or introduce you to life-enhancing experiences. You likely hold their recommendations in high regard because they have consistently proven their ability to offer valuable insights.

Empowering Decision-Making

Your recommendations empower your friends in their decision-making processes. Life is filled with choices, and your suggestions can make those choices more manageable. Whether it is choosing a new book to read, deciding to explore a new hobby, or adopting a healthier lifestyle, your guidance provides clarity.

Imagine a friend who is contemplating a career change and feeling overwhelmed by the options. If you recommend a book on career development or share insights from your own professional journey, you provide them with a valuable resource to navigate this significant decision.

Sparking New Interests and Passions

Recommendations have the potential to spark new interests and passions in your friends' lives. They can introduce them to subjects, hobbies, or activities they may not have considered otherwise. Your suggestion can be the spark that ignites a new passion.

For instance, if you recommend a documentary about a niche topic you are passionate about, your friends might watch it out of curiosity. In doing so, they could discover a new interest that brings them joy and fulfillment. Your recommendation becomes the gateway to a world of possibilities.

Supporting Personal Growth

Your recommendations actively support your friends' personal growth journeys. Whether it is suggesting self-help books, online courses, or personal development seminars, your guidance equips them with tools and resources to evolve and thrive.

Consider how recommendations for wellness practices, such as meditation, yoga, or journaling, can enhance your friends' mental and emotional well-being. By sharing these practices, you contribute to their personal growth and resilience.

Strengthening Connections

The act of recommending something is a gesture of care and connection. It shows that you are invested in your friends' well-being and growth. This strengthens the bonds of friendship and fosters a sense of community.

When you recommend a book or resource, you are essentially saying, "I believe this can benefit you, and I want to share it with you." This act of sharing creates a sense of togetherness and reinforces the idea that you are on this journey of self-improvement and growth together.

Encouraging Positive Habits

Your recommendations can also encourage the adoption of positive habits. Whether it is suggesting a daily gratitude journal, a morning exercise routine, or a habit-tracking app, you contribute to the cultivation of behaviors that promote well-being.

Positive habits often require a gentle nudge or initial guidance. Your recommendations provide that nudge, helping your friends establish routines that enhance their physical, mental, and emotional health. Over time, these habits can lead to lasting positive change.

Creating Conversations and Connections

Recommendations create opportunities for meaningful conversations and connections. When your friends explore the resources or practices you suggest, it opens doors to discussions about their experiences and insights.

For instance, if you recommend a thought-provoking podcast episode, your friends might listen to it and then share their thoughts with you. This exchange of ideas and perspectives deepens your connections and broadens your collective understanding.

The Ripple Effect of Positive Change

In conclusion, your recommendations have the potential to set in motion a ripple effect of positive change in your friends' lives. Each suggestion you make, whether it is a book, a piece of advice, or an idea, carries the potential to inspire, educate, and empower.

As you continue to share your recommendations, remember that you are not just offering suggestions; you are planting seeds of growth, curiosity, and well-being in the lives of those you care about. Your influence, driven by your genuine desire to support their journeys, can lead to remarkable transformations and lasting positive change.

So, go ahead and share your recommendations with enthusiasm and sincerity, for you have the power to spark positive change in the lives of your friends and contribute to a collective journey of growth and self-discovery.

• Invite your friends and loved ones to read and share this book, creating a ripple of positivity.

The Power of Shared Knowledge

Inviting your friends and loved ones to read and share this book is akin to extending an invitation to embark on a transformative journey together. It is an invitation to explore the boundless potential of personal growth, self-discovery, and positive change collectively.

Fostering a Community of Growth

When you invite others to join you in reading and discussing this book, you are essentially fostering a community of growth and self-improvement. You create a shared space where individuals can come together to explore ideas, share insights, and support one another on their respective journeys.

Consider the profound impact of a community that shares a common goal of personal development and well-being. It becomes a place of encouragement, inspiration, and camaraderie. Together, you and your friends can navigate the chapters of this book and, in doing so, navigate the chapters of your lives with greater purpose.

The Ripple Effect of Positivity

The act of sharing this book with friends and loved ones initiates a ripple effect of positivity that can extend far beyond your immediate circle. Here is how this ripple effect takes shape:

1. **Inspiring Growth:** As your friends and loved ones begin to read the book, they are exposed to valuable insights and practical wisdom. These insights can inspire personal growth and encourage them to explore new paths of self-improvement.

2. **Sparking Conversations:** Reading the book together gives rise to meaningful conversations. You and your friends can discuss the book's teachings, share your interpretations, and reflect on how its principles apply to your lives. These conversations can lead to deeper self-awareness and shared growth.

3. **Shared Experiences:** When you share a book with someone, you are essentially sharing an experience. This

shared experience creates a sense of connection and unity among you and your friends. It reinforces the idea that you are all on a collective journey of self-discovery and positive change.

4. **Supportive Network:** Reading and discussing the book together establishes a support network. It means that you have a group of individuals who are invested in your well-being and growth, just as you are invested in theirs. This network can provide encouragement, motivation, and accountability.

5. **Multiplying Impact:** As your friends and loved ones experience personal growth and positive change through the book, they, in turn, may be inspired to share it with their own circles. This multiplication effect spreads the message of positivity and personal development to a wider audience, creating a ripple that continues to expand.

Shared Insights and Personal Growth

Inviting others to read and share this book opens the door to shared insights and personal growth. Each individual brings their unique perspective and life experiences to the discussions. As a result, the book's teachings may resonate differently with each person, leading to diverse interpretations and revelations.

These shared insights enrich the reading experience. They allow you and your friends to gain a deeper understanding of the book's principles and how they can be applied in various life contexts. The collective exploration of the book becomes a journey of mutual learning and self-discovery.

Strengthening Relationships

Sharing this book with your friends and loved ones has the potential to strengthen your relationships in profound ways. It deepens the bonds of connection by providing a shared interest and a common purpose. You embark on a shared intellectual and emotional journey, which can foster greater understanding and empathy among you.

Consider the joy of engaging in meaningful discussions with your friends about the book's teachings. These conversations create opportunities for vulnerability, self-expression, and mutual support. They allow you to see one another's growth and transformation, strengthening your relationships in the process.

Creating a Culture of Positivity

When you and your friends read and share this book, you contribute to the creation of a culture of positivity and personal growth within your circle. This culture is characterized by a shared commitment to self-improvement, well-being, and the pursuit of a fulfilling life.

In a culture of positivity, individuals uplift one another. They celebrate each other's achievements, offer support during challenges, and share in the collective joy of personal growth. This culture permeates your interactions and interactions with others, spreading its influence far and wide.

The Gift of Transformation

In essence, inviting your friends and loved ones to read and share this book is a gift of transformation. It is a gift that has the potential to spark profound positive changes in their lives. As they embark on this journey of self-discovery and personal growth, they may uncover hidden strengths, overcome challenges, and **unlock their fullest potential.**

Imagine the satisfaction of knowing that you played a part in facilitating such transformation in the lives of those you care about. Your invitation becomes an act of kindness and empowerment, a gesture that has the power to shape destinies and inspire greatness.

In Conclusion

In conclusion, inviting your friends and loved ones to read and share this book is an act of generosity and a catalyst for personal and collective growth. It initiates a ripple of positivity that touches hearts, minds, and lives. It strengthens relationships, fosters a culture of well-being, and creates opportunities for shared learning and transformation.

As you extend this invitation, remember that you are not just recommending a book; you are extending an invitation to a journey of self-discovery, growth, and positive change. You are igniting a spark that has the potential to illuminate the path to a brighter, more fulfilling future for you and your loved ones.

So, with enthusiasm and a sense of purpose, invite your friends and loved ones to read and share this book. Embrace the journey together and may the ripple of positivity you create continue to expand, touching countless lives along the way.

~ ~ ~ ~ ~ ~ ~ ~ ~ ~

Acknowledgments:
• Give a shoutout to your own contributors and supporters who made this journey possible for you.

"On a personal note, I have experienced the ups and downs of what I sometimes refer to as my 'roller coaster' life. This journey has included significant challenges, such as the sudden loss of my spouse in 2012, the unexpected passing of my dearest friend of 44 years in 2023, and deliberate choices like relinquishing my passion for wine-making. Throughout it all, I've been fortunate to have unwavering support from my family and friends, who have stood by me during the lows, celebrated with me during the highs, and embraced every moment in between."

Always Grateful,

KJJM

Acknowledging Your Champions

As you reflect upon your journey through life and this remarkable book, it is essential to recognize and express gratitude to those who have played pivotal roles in shaping your path. These individuals, often your champions, are the ones who have offered support, encouragement, and inspiration at various stages of your life.

Family: The Foundation of Support

Family is often the cornerstone of our support system. They are the ones who stand by us through thick and thin, offering unconditional love and unwavering support. Your parents, siblings, and extended family have undoubtedly been instrumental in your life's journey.

Take a moment to think about the lessons you have learned from your family, the values instilled in you, and the countless sacrifices made on your behalf. These are the threads that weave the tapestry of your life. Your family's support and belief in you have provided the foundation upon which you have built your aspirations and achievements.

Friends: The Pillars of Friendship

Friends are the pillars of friendship, offering camaraderie, laughter, and a shoulder to lean on. They are the ones who celebrate your successes and stand by your side during challenges. Your friends have been with you through life's ups and downs, creating cherished memories along the way.

Consider the friends who have walked alongside you in this journey called life. They have been sounding boards for your ideas, confidants for your secrets, and companions in your adventures. Their unwavering friendship has added depth and color to your experiences.

Mentors: Guiding Lights

Mentors are the guiding lights who illuminate the path to personal and professional growth. They are individuals who have shared their wisdom, knowledge, and expertise, helping you navigate the complexities of life. Whether in your career, hobbies, or personal development, mentors have been instrumental in your journey.

Reflect on the mentors who have shaped your life. They may be teachers, coaches, colleagues, or anyone who has imparted valuable insights and guidance. Their mentorship has equipped you with the tools and wisdom to overcome obstacles and achieve your goals.

Teachers: Nurturing Minds

Teachers play a pivotal role in nurturing young minds and fostering a love for learning. They are the ones who have educated and inspired you, shaping your intellect and curiosity. Teachers have ignited the spark of knowledge within you, setting you on a path of continuous learning.

Think about the teachers who have made a lasting impact on your life. They may have taught you in school, guided you in extracurricular activities, or served as mentors in your academic pursuits. Their dedication to education has contributed to your growth and development.

Colleagues: Collaborative Allies

Colleagues are collaborative allies in your professional journey. They are the individuals with whom you have worked side by side, sharing ideas, solving challenges, and achieving collective goals. Colleagues have been integral to your career progression and success.

Consider the colleagues with whom you have had the privilege of working. They have provided support, collaboration, and camaraderie in the workplace. Their teamwork and shared vision have contributed to your accomplishments and the growth of your career.

Community: The Collective Support

Community represents the collective support of individuals who share common interests, values, or goals. It is a network of people who come together to create a sense of belonging and unity. Communities have provided you with a sense of identity and purpose.

Reflect on the various communities to which you belong. They may include cultural groups, social organizations, or associations centered around shared interests. These communities have enriched your life by fostering connections, shared experiences, and a sense of belonging.

Supporters: Encouraging Believers

Supporters are the individuals who have believed in you, cheered you on, and provided encouragement even in the face of challenges. They are the ones who have recognized your potential and offered unwavering support on your journey.

Think about the supporters who have stood by your side, offering words of encouragement, motivation, and belief in your abilities. Their unwavering faith in you has been a source of inspiration, propelling you forward even when self-doubt crept in.

The Power of Gratitude

Gratitude is a powerful emotion that has the capacity to deepen connections and inspire acts of kindness. Expressing gratitude to your contributors and supporters is not only a gesture of appreciation but also an acknowledgment of the profound impact they have had on your life.

When you convey your gratitude, whether through words or actions, you strengthen the bonds of connection. You let your champions know that their support has not gone unnoticed and that their presence in your life is cherished. Gratitude fosters a culture of appreciation and reciprocity, creating a positive cycle of giving and receiving.

The Ripple Effect of Gratitude

Gratitude is not limited to a one-time expression; it has a ripple effect that extends far beyond its initial gesture. When you express gratitude to your contributors and supporters, you inspire them to continue their acts of kindness and support. Your acknowledgment reinforces the value of their contributions and encourages them to be catalysts for positive change in the lives of others.

Consider the profound impact of your gratitude on those you acknowledge. Your words or actions may uplift their spirits, validate their efforts, and motivate them to continue their support. As a result, the ripple-effects of gratitude continues to expand, touching countless lives along the way.

Embracing a Grateful Heart

Embracing a grateful heart is a lifelong practice that enriches your own life and the lives of those around you. It allows you to recognize the abundance of support and love that surrounds you, even in the midst of challenges. Gratitude opens the door to deeper connections, greater happiness, and a more meaningful life.

As you celebrate the contributors and supporters who have made your journey possible, take a moment to reflect on the profound impact they have had on your life.

Consider how their support, guidance, and belief in you have shaped your path and contributed to your growth and accomplishments.

Expressing Your Gratitude

Expressing gratitude can take many forms, and you can choose the approach that feels most authentic to you. Whether through heartfelt conversations, handwritten notes, acts of kindness, or dedicatory gestures, the key is to convey your appreciation sincerely and genuinely.

A Shoutout to Your Champions

In this chapter, let your heart overflow with gratitude as you give a shoutout to your champions. Acknowledge their contributions and support and let them know how profoundly grateful you are for their presence in your life. Your shoutout is not only a tribute to them but also a testament to the power of connection, support, and gratitude in shaping a life filled with purpose and fulfillment.

Continuing the Journey Together

As you express your gratitude, remember that your journey is ongoing. Life is a continuous exploration of growth, connections, and shared experiences. Your champions will continue to play significant roles in your life, and your relationships will evolve as you embark on new chapters.

Invite your champions to join you in continuing this journey together. Share your aspirations, dreams, and goals with them, and encourage them to do the same. Embrace the power of collective support and collaboration, knowing that together, you can inspire positive change and create a legacy of shared experiences and achievements.

A Heartfelt Thank You

To your family, friends, mentors, teachers, colleagues, community, supporters, and all those who have contributed to your journey, this is a heartfelt thank you. Your support, belief, and presence have made all the difference. Your contributions have enriched your life's narrative and added depth to your experiences.

As you express your gratitude, may you find joy in the act of acknowledgment and fulfillment in the knowledge that you are surrounded by champions who believe in you. Together, you have created a tapestry of support, love, and shared moments that continue to weave the beautiful story of your life.

Celebrating Your Journey

In closing, take a moment to celebrate your journey—the highs and lows, the triumphs and challenges, the connections, and contributions. Your journey is a testament to the power of human connection and the profound impact of gratitude. May you continue to embrace each moment, express your appreciation, and celebrate the champions who have made your life's journey a remarkable and meaningful one.

• Express gratitude to those who have been part of your journey.

The Gratitude Journey

Gratitude is more than just a polite gesture or a social nicety. It is a profound and deeply human experience that transcends cultures and generations. At its core, gratitude is about recognizing the goodness in our lives and the kindness of others. It is about appreciating the countless moments, big and small, that have shaped our journey.

The journey of gratitude begins with self-awareness. It involves taking a moment to pause, reflect, and genuinely acknowledge the positive impact that individuals and experiences have had on our lives. It is a journey of looking inward to understand how our hearts have been touched, and outward to express our appreciation.

The Champions of Our Journey

Our journey through life is marked by encounters with remarkable individuals who become the champions of our story. These champions come in various forms, each contributing their unique qualities to our narrative.

Family: The Pillars of Love

Family is often the bedrock of our support system. They are the ones who have been with us from the very beginning, sharing our joys and comforting us in times of sorrow. Family members provide unconditional love, nurturing, and a sense of belonging.

Consider your parents, siblings, and extended family members. They have been your constants, offering guidance, encouragement, and unwavering support. Their love has shaped your identity and provided the foundation upon which you have built your life.

Friends: The Keepers of Memories

Friends are the keepers of memories and the companions of our adventures. They are the ones with whom we have shared laughter, secrets, and life's ups and downs. Friends enrich our lives with their camaraderie and understanding.

Think about the friends who have walked alongside you on this journey called life. They have celebrated your successes, lent a listening ear during challenges, and created cherished memories together. Their friendships have added color and depth to your experiences.

Mentors: Guiding Lights

Mentors are the guiding lights who illuminate our path to growth and self-discovery. They are individuals who have shared their wisdom, knowledge, and expertise, helping us navigate the complexities of life. Mentors inspire us to reach higher and become the best versions of ourselves.

Reflect on the mentors who have shaped your journey. They may have been teachers, coaches, colleagues, or anyone who has imparted valuable insights and guidance. Their mentorship has equipped you with the tools and wisdom to overcome obstacles and achieve your goals.

Teachers: Nurturers of Curiosity

Teachers are the nurturers of curiosity and the cultivators of knowledge. They ignite the spark of learning within us, instilling a love for education and inquiry. Teachers play a pivotal role in shaping our intellect and nurturing our thirst for knowledge.

Consider the teachers who have left a lasting impact on your life. They may have been your educators in school, mentors in extracurricular activities, or guides in your academic pursuits. Their dedication to education has contributed to your growth and development.

Colleagues: Collaborators in Success

Colleagues are collaborative allies in our professional journey. They are the individuals with whom we have worked side by side, sharing ideas, solving challenges, and achieving collective goals. Colleagues have been integral to our career progression and success.

Think about the colleagues with whom you have had the privilege of working. They have provided support, collaboration, and camaraderie in the workplace. Their teamwork and shared vision have contributed to your accomplishments and the growth of your career.

Community: The Tapestry of Belonging

Community represents the tapestry of belonging and the power of collective support. It is a network of individuals who come together based on common interests, values, or goals. Communities provide us with a sense of identity, purpose, and shared experiences.

Reflect on the various communities to which you belong. They may include cultural groups, social organizations, or associations centered around shared interests. These communities have enriched your life by fostering connections, shared experiences, and a sense of belonging.

Supporters: Believers in Our Potential

Supporters are the believers in our potential and the encouragers of our dreams. They are the individuals who have stood by our side, offering words of encouragement, motivation, and belief in our abilities. Supporters have been instrumental in our journey.

Consider the supporters who have cheered you on, believed in your capabilities, and provided unwavering encouragement. Their belief in you has been a source of inspiration, propelling you forward even when self-doubt crept in.

The Impact of Gratitude

Expressing gratitude is not merely a polite gesture; it has the power to profoundly impact our lives and the lives of those we acknowledge. When we convey our gratitude sincerely and authentically, several remarkable things happen:

1. **Deepening Connections**: Gratitude strengthens the bonds of connection with those we appreciate. It fosters a sense of belonging and reinforces the value of our relationships.

2. **Uplifting Spirits**: When we express gratitude, we uplift the spirits of those we acknowledge. It brings joy, validation, and a sense of fulfillment to their lives.

3. **Motivating Kindness**: Gratitude has a ripple effect. When we express appreciation, we inspire acts of kindness and support from others, creating a cycle of giving and receiving.

4. **Strengthening Resilience**: Gratitude cultivates resilience by helping us focus on the positive aspects of life, even during challenging times. It shifts our perspective and fosters emotional well-being.

5. **Fostering Happiness**: Gratitude is linked to greater happiness and life satisfaction. It reminds us of the abundance in our lives and encourages a positive outlook.

Expressions of Gratitude

Expressing gratitude can take various forms, and we can choose the approach that resonates most with us and our recipients. Here are some meaningful ways to convey our appreciation:

1. **Heartfelt Conversations**: Engaging in heartfelt conversations allows us to express our gratitude directly and authentically. It is an opportunity to share our feelings and appreciation with sincerity.

2. **Handwritten Notes**: A handwritten note or letter carries a personal touch and is a timeless way to convey gratitude. It allows us to craft our words carefully and express our feelings on paper.

3. **Acts of Kindness**: Performing acts of kindness is a way to show our appreciation through actions. Small gestures, such as helping with tasks or offering support, can speak volumes.

4. **Dedicatory Gestures**: Dedication of achievements, projects, or efforts to someone who has contributed significantly is a meaningful way to express gratitude publicly.

5. **Tokens of Appreciation**: Gifts or tokens of appreciation, chosen thoughtfully, can convey our gratitude effectively. These gifts serve as tangible reminders of our appreciation.

6. **Expressions of Thanks**: Simply saying "thank you" sincerely and frequently is a powerful way to express gratitude in everyday interactions.

The Art of Acknowledgment

Acknowledging the contributions and support of those who have been part of our journey is an art that can be practiced and honed. Here are some tips for effectively expressing gratitude:

1. **Be Specific**: When expressing gratitude, be specific about what you are thankful for. Mention the actions, qualities, or moments that have had a meaningful impact.

2. **Be Sincere**: Authenticity is key. Express your gratitude with sincerity, and let your words come from the heart. Genuine appreciation is felt and appreciated in return.

3. **Timing Matters**: Express gratitude in a timely manner. Do not wait too long to acknowledge someone's contribution, as it may lose its impact.

4. **Consider Personal Preferences**: Tailor your expression of gratitude to the recipient's preferences. Some individuals may appreciate public acknowledgment, while others may prefer private gestures.

5. **Reciprocate Kindness**: If someone has supported you, consider ways to reciprocate their kindness. Acts of kindness can create a cycle of appreciation and support.

The Ripple Effect of Gratitude

Expressing gratitude not only enriches our lives but also creates a ripple effect that extends far beyond our immediate relationships.

When we acknowledge and appreciate others, we inspire a culture of gratitude and kindness in our communities and society as a whole.

Our expressions of gratitude can motivate others to take similar actions, creating a chain reaction of positivity and generosity. It fosters a sense of interconnectedness and reminds us that our actions have the power to uplift and inspire those around us.

Inviting Others to Express Gratitude

As we embrace the practice of gratitude, we can also invite others to express their appreciation. Encouraging friends, family, colleagues, and acquaintances to acknowledge and appreciate the positive impact of those around them creates a culture of gratitude and mutual appreciation.

Gratitude as a Lifelong Practice

Gratitude is not a one-time event but a lifelong practice. It is an ongoing journey of recognizing the goodness in our lives and expressing our appreciation. As we continue our journey, we will encounter new champions, experience new moments of grace, and find countless reasons to be grateful.

A Heartfelt Thank You

To those who have been part of our journey, this is a heartfelt thank you. Your support, belief, and presence have made all the difference. Your contributions have enriched our life's narrative and added depth to our experiences.

Continuing the Journey Together

As we express our gratitude, let us remember that our journey is ongoing. Life is a continuous exploration of growth, connections, and shared experiences. Our champions will continue to play significant roles in our lives, and our relationships will evolve as we embark on new chapters.

Invite your champions to join you in continuing this journey together. Share your aspirations, dreams, and goals with them, and encourage them to do the same. Embrace the power of collective support and collaboration, knowing that together, you can inspire positive change and create a legacy of shared experiences and achievements.

Celebrating Our Journey

In closing, take a moment to celebrate our journey—the highs and lows, the triumphs and challenges, the connections, and contributions. Our journey is a testament to the power of human connection and the profound impact of gratitude. May we continue to embrace each moment, express our appreciation, and celebrate the champions who have made our life's journey a remarkable and meaningful one.

- **Invite your loved ones and friends to join in this journey of gratitude – the more, the merrier.**

The Gift of Gratitude Shared

Gratitude is a gift that becomes even more precious when shared. When we invite our loved ones and friends to embark on this journey with us, we extend the opportunity for them to experience the profound benefits of gratitude in their own lives. It is like sharing a secret recipe for happiness and fulfillment.

Why Invite Others on the Gratitude Journey?

1. **Strengthening Bonds**: When we invite our loved ones to join us on the journey of gratitude, we strengthen the bonds of our relationships. Expressing appreciation and acknowledgment creates a sense of connection and deepens our emotional ties.

2. **Creating a Culture of Gratitude**: By encouraging our friends and family to practice gratitude, we contribute to the creation of a culture of gratitude within our social circles. This culture promotes positivity, kindness, and mutual appreciation.

3. **Enhancing Well-Being**: Gratitude has been linked to enhanced well-being and emotional health. When we share the practice of gratitude, we contribute to the overall happiness and positive mental health of our loved ones.

4. **Inspiring Kindness**: Expressing gratitude often inspires acts of kindness and generosity. **When we invite others to join us in acknowledging the goodness in their lives, we motivate them to pay it forward and spread positivity.**

5. **Deepening Understanding**: The practice of gratitude encourages us to see life from a more appreciative perspective. When we invite our loved ones to engage in this practice, we deepen their understanding of the beauty in everyday moments.

How to Invite Others on the Gratitude Journey

1. **Lead by Example**: The most powerful way to invite others on the gratitude journey is by leading by example. Begin your own practice of gratitude, and let your friends and family witness the positive changes it brings to your life.

2. **Share Your Experiences**: Talk about your own experiences with gratitude. Share how it has impacted your life, improved your outlook, and enriched your relationships. Personal stories can be inspiring.

3. **Offer Gratitude Challenges**: Encourage your loved ones to participate in gratitude challenges with you. These challenges can involve daily or weekly expressions of gratitude. Challenge each other to find new things to appreciate.

4. **Start a Gratitude Journal Together**: Consider starting a gratitude journal with a friend or family member. Share your daily or weekly entries and discuss the moments of gratitude you have recorded.

5. **Express Appreciation**: Take the time to express your appreciation directly to your loved ones. Let them know how much you value their presence in your life and how grateful you are for their support.

6. **Recommend Gratitude Resources**: Share books, articles, podcasts, or apps related to gratitude with your friends and family. These resources can provide guidance and inspiration for their own gratitude practice.

7. **Celebrate Gratitude Together**: Host a gratitude-themed gathering or event. It could be a dinner where everyone shares something they are grateful for or a gratitude-themed game night.

8. **Create a Gratitude Ritual**: Establish a gratitude ritual that you can practice together. Whether it is a weekly phone call to share moments of gratitude or a monthly gratitude circle, having a shared practice can be powerful.

The Ripple Effect of Shared Gratitude

When we invite our loved ones and friends to join us on the gratitude journey, we create a ripple effect of positivity and appreciation. The impact of shared gratitude extends beyond our immediate relationships and influences our communities and society as a whole.

As our loved ones experience the benefits of gratitude, they, in turn, may invite others to join them on this journey. This creates a beautiful cycle of appreciation and kindness, where the practice of gratitude spreads like wildfire, touching the lives of many.

Gratitude as a Lifelong Journey

Gratitude is not a one-time event but a lifelong journey. It is an ongoing practice that evolves with us as we navigate the various chapters of our lives. As we continue this journey with our loved ones and friends, we will encounter new moments of appreciation, discover new reasons to be grateful, and deepen our connections.

A Heartfelt Invitation

To our loved ones and friends, this is a heartfelt invitation to embark on the journey of gratitude with us. Your presence in our lives is cherished, and we believe that practicing gratitude together can enhance the beauty of our relationships and the richness of our experiences.

Continuing the Journey Together

As we share this practice of gratitude, let us remember that our journey is ongoing. Life is a continuous exploration of growth, connections, and shared moments. Together, we can embrace each moment, express our appreciation, and create a legacy of mutual appreciation and happiness.

Celebrating Our Shared Journey

In closing, take a moment to celebrate our shared journey—the journey of gratitude, the journey of connection, and the journey of positivity. Our willingness to invite others to join us in this practice is a testament to the depth of our relationships and the power of gratitude. May we continue to inspire each other, uplift each other, and share the beauty of gratitude with the world.

~ ~ ~ ~ ~ ~ ~ ~ ~ ~

Appendix:

- **Explore additional resources for your personal growth, and do not hesitate to share them with friends.**
- **Recommend books and references that have enriched your life and learning.**

1. **Books:**

⬥ "The Power of Habit" by Charles Duhigg: Explore the science of habit formation and how to change it.

⬥ "Daring Greatly" by Brené Brown: Learn about vulnerability, courage, and the importance of embracing imperfections.

⬥ "Atomic Habits" by James Clear: Discover strategies for building good habits, breaking bad ones, and mastering the tiny behaviors that lead to remarkable results.

⬥ "Mindset: The New Psychology of Success" by Carol S. Dweck: Explore the concept of mindset and how it impacts success and personal growth.

2. **Online Courses:**

⬥ Coursera (www.coursera.org[1]): Offers a wide range of courses on personal development, leadership, and emotional intelligence.

---

1. http://www.coursera.org/

◈ Udemy (www.udemy.com[2]): Provides courses on various personal growth topics, from time management to mindfulness.

◈ LinkedIn Learning (www.linkedin.com/learning): Features courses on leadership, communication skills, and self-improvement.

3. Podcasts:

◈ "The Tony Robbins Podcast": Tony Robbins shares strategies for personal and professional growth.

◈ "The Tim Ferriss Show": Tim Ferriss interviews world-class performers to extract their best tactics, tools, and routines.

◈ "The School of Greatness" by Lewis Howes: Explores the stories and strategies of inspiring individuals.

4. Mentorship:
◈ Seek out mentors in your field of interest or personal growth. Mentorship can provide personalized guidance and support.

5. Workshops and Seminars:
◈ Look for local workshops and seminars on topics like leadership, emotional intelligence, and goal setting.

6. Apps and Tools:

◈ Headspace: A meditation app for mindfulness and stress reduction.

◈ Habitica: A gamified app that helps you build and maintain good habits.

---

2. http://www.udemy.com/

◈ Duolingo: Learn a new language and expand your horizons.

7. **Support Groups:**

◈ Explore local or online support groups focused on areas such as mental health, addiction recovery, or personal development.

8. **Professional Training:**

◈ Depending on your career goals, professional training or certification programs can enhance your skills and knowledge.

9. **Blogs and Websites:**

◈ Medium (www.medium.com[3]): A platform where experts share articles on personal growth, self-improvement, and motivation.

◈ TED Talks (www.ted.com[4]): Features inspiring talks on a wide range of topics.

10. **Community Events:**

◈ Attend community events, workshops, or seminars related to personal growth and self-improvement.

Remember that personal growth is a highly individualized journey, and different resources may resonate with different people. It is important to explore and discover what works best for you. Additionally, sharing these resources with friends can lead to meaningful discussions and collective growth.

~ ~ ~ ~ ~ ~ ~ ~ ~ ~

---

3. http://www.medium.com/

4. http://www.ted.com/

Dedication

Let this book be a source of inspiration, connection, and growth, both for you, your loved ones, and the friends you choose to share it with.

Always grateful,
Kevin James Joseph McNamara

~ ~

#KevinJamesJosephMcNamara
#KevinJJosephMcNamara
#KevinJJMcNamara

#70ish, #80ish, #90ish, #100ish or More
And this book is for me!